Love poetry
in sixteenth-century France

For my mother

Stephen Minta

Love Poetry
in sixteenth-century France

*A study in themes
and traditions*

Manchester
University Press

First published 1977 by
Manchester University Press
Oxford Road, Manchester M13 9PL

ISBN 0 7190 0676 7

British Library cataloguing in publication data

Minta, Stephen
    Love poetry in sixteenth-century France.
    1. French poetry—16th century—History and criticism 2. Love poetry,
French—History and criticism
    I. Title
    841'.3'09354   PQ155.L7

ISBN 0-7190-0676-7

Printed in Great Britain
at the Alden Press, Oxford

Contents

Acknowledgements

My thanks are due first of all to Professor M. M. McGowan, with whom I worked on sixteenth-century French poetry at the University of Sussex; to Professor I. D. McFarlane of the University of Oxford, for help on a number of occasions and for the use of his complete word index to Maurice Scève's *Délie*; to Professor R. A. Hallett of the College of William and Mary in Virginia, for permission to make use of his translation of the *Délie*; to the Centre National de la Recherche Scientifique, for a grant which made part of the research for this book possible; to the editor of *French Studies*, for permission to make use of my article 'A problem of literary history: "Petrarchism" in early sixteenth-century French poetry', published by that journal in 1976 (vol. 30, pp. 140–52); Hutchinson Publishing Group Ltd and Harper and Row Inc., for permission to quote from P. Dronke, *The Medieval Lyric*; and Yale University Press, for permission to quote from *The Literature of Ancient Egypt*, edited by W. K. Simpson.

Translations

I have not adopted a wholly consistent attitude to the translation of passages in foreign languages. I have, however, translated all the important passages of Italian and Occitanian poetry that I have used. I have not in general translated prose texts in foreign languages, as this would have been too demanding of space. In the central chapters of this book I have included translations of the more difficult dizains of the *Délie*, since I thought this might be of help to readers approaching Scève for the first time. All such translations from the *Délie* are by Ronald Hallett; all other translations are my own.

Introduction

In this book I have tried to provide some answers to a question that is often asked: why is it that the love poetry of the Pléiade is of such importance in the history of French literature? To this end I have given as clear an account as I can of the state of French love poetry in the years preceding the publication of du Bellay's *Olive* (1549), a work which, for all the criticisms which have been levelled against it, seems to me the first in the sixteenth century to indicate a radical change of attitude and of taste. It is not easy to write about the poetry of this period, for there is such an apparent maze of themes and influences to be explored, such an enormously long lyric tradition stretching back beyond the psychologically desirable starting point of 1500, that often one has the impression it will never be possible to begin anywhere. My own interest in literary traditions stems from a reading of Maurice Scève's *Délie*, a collection of 449 poems first published in Lyon in 1544, and a glance at that collection will reveal the nature of the problems facing the literary historian. As Professor I. D. McFarlane writes in his edition of the work:

> *Délie* draws on a literary idiom or *fonds commun* which has been fed by the Grands Rhétoriqueurs, the classics, Italian poetry, themes popularised by the Neo-latin poets as well as by those writing in the vernacular, a certain philosophical spiritualism (associated more especially with the name of Ficino), and what is loosely called the 'Alexandrian' tradition.[1]

What is one to make of that? It has long seemed to me that any attempt to isolate the specific contribution of each of these forces to the poetry of the sixteenth century would be a hopeless task, for the mixing which has taken place is far too complex to be resolved. And so it has been one of the aims of this book to divert critical attention away from specific questions of the transmission of themes and the identification of sources, in order to give a more general, and I hope a more interesting, idea of what it was like to work within the poetic tradition which the

1

sixteenth century inherited. Against this background the significance of the innovations which the Pléiade introduced should emerge quite naturally.

Perhaps the most important aspect of early sixteenth-century love poetry in France is the extent to which it is dependent on the medieval courtly tradition. That is to say, there is a marked continuity in French poetry which links the work of Marot (1496–1544) to that of Machaut (c. 1300–77) and beyond it to the lyrics of the earliest trouvères. This is a point which frequently passes unobserved, largely, I suspect, because of the traditional division between Medieval and Renaissance studies. Professor C. A. Mayer, for example, has suggested that Marot's love poems are significant since they appear to show some of the earliest signs of Italian influence on French literature. But the themes which Marot employs are not specifically Italian at all: they belong just as much to the world of traditional French courtly poetry. Of course one finds the same themes in the Italian tradition and in the French, but that is in the nature of love poetry itself. What the poets share from a thematic point of view is infinitely less interesting than those things which they do not share, and I do not think one could ever make satisfactory judgements about a writer's significance on the basis of themes alone.

The problems which the courtly movement presents to any critic who attempts to be too specific in matters of influence and tradition are well illustrated in Peter Dronke's *Medieval Latin and the Rise of European Love-Lyric*. In his rejection of the notion that courtly love was a southern French invention, dating from the end of the eleventh century, that it was, in C. S. Lewis's often quoted words, a 'new feeling', Dronke argues that it is, on the contrary, a feeling so widespread that it can scarcely be said to have any origins at all. He proposes the following:

(i) that 'the new feeling' of *amour courtois* is at least as old as Egypt of the second millennium B.C., and might indeed occur at any time or place: that it is, as Professor Marrou suspected, 'un secteur du cœur, un des aspects éternels de l'homme';

(ii) that the feeling of *amour courtois* is not confined to courtly or chivalric socievty, but is reflected even in the earliest recorded popular verse of Europe (which almost certainly had a long oral tradition behind it);

(iii) that researches into European courtly poetry should
      therefore be concerned with the variety of sophisticated
      and learned *development* of *courtois* themes, not with
      seeking specific origins for the themes themselves.[2]

An eager search for origins is, I would suggest, as inappropriate
to the study of sixteenth-century poetry as it is to the study of
the earliest courtly lyrics. 'The language of love', as J. Hutton
wrote, 'tends to be everywhere the same'.[3] For an illustration of
this one could look at the popular courtly theme which views
love as a kind of sickness, a theme frequently accompanied by
the notion that it is a sickness which only the beloved can cure.
Its dissemination throughout the European tradition is well
known and it is capable of variation on many levels; it may be
used to express anything from the most spiritual desires to the
most carnal, and is indeed often employed with a deliberately
ambiguous intent in common with many of the stock themes
and images associated with the lyric tradition. To search for the
'origins' of the theme would be a vain task indeed, for it appears
already well established among the love songs of the Egyptian
New Kingdom (1570–1085 B.C.). Any medieval love poet in
Europe would have felt quite at home with lines like these:

> Now I'll lie down inside
> and act as if I'm sick.
> My neighbors will come in to visit,
> and with them my girl.
> She'll put the doctors out,
> for she's the one to know my hurt.

or:

> Seven days have passed, and I've not seen my lady love;
> a sickness has shot through me . . .
> If the best surgeons come to me,
> my heart will not be comforted with their remedies . . .
> Telling me 'she's come' is what will bring me back to life.
> It's only her name which will raise me up . . .
> To me the lady love is more remedial than any potion.[4]

Over two thousand years later we find the theme unchanged.
Peter Dronke quotes the following lines from the Arabic poet
At-Tutili, who was born in Tudela, near Zaragoza in Spain,
and who died in A.D. 1126:

Meu 'l-habib enfermo de meu amar—
quen ad sanar?
Bi nafsi amante, que sed a meu legar!

My dearest one is sick with love of me—
who will his doctor be?
By my love's soul, how he waits, thirstily![5]

These lines, recognisably Spanish, though with Arabic additions (*habib* = 'beloved', *nafs* = 'soul'), belong to a fascinating poetic tradition which was discovered by Samuel Stern in 1948, the tradition of the bilingual *muwashshah*. The *muwashshah* is an Arabic strophic poem, the earliest examples of which date from the eleventh century, but the origins of which may go back as far as the year A.D. 900. The form was invented in Spain during the period of Arab domination, and in subject-matter, language, and style it belongs entirely to the classical Arabic tradition. But the poem ends with a coda or *kharja* which may be written in colloquial Arabic, or in Spanish, or, as in the above example, in a mixture of both. And it is interesting to note that these codas in fact preserve the earliest surviving secular lyrics in a Romance tongue.

In the sixteenth century the popularity of the theme of love as a sickness is in no way diminished, and many of the other themes which are popular in Renaissance poetry have similarly long histories behind them. In the Egyptian love songs, for example, one already finds references to the beloved's hair or eyes as weapons of enticement and domination:

With her hair she throws lassoes at me,
with her eyes she catches me,
with her necklace entangles me
and with her seal ring brands me.

[p. 324]

Reference to the seal ring immediately recalls numerous poems on such subjects in Italian or French, while the antithetical treatment of love which is again so common in the European tradition finds a place in the Egyptian songs also as evidenced in the following lines, spoken by a woman at the moment of parting from her lover:

If I see sugar cakes,
[they are to me like] salt;

    sweet pomegranate wine in my mouth
    is as bitter as the gall of birds.

[pp. 303–4]

Even the convention by which the beloved is called 'sister', a convention which in the European tradition goes back as far as the Song of Songs, has an exact parallel in the Egyptian poetic tradition. What is always important, therefore, is not to determine which particular images were borrowed and from whom, but to try to recover a sense of the continuity of the lyric tradition one is dealing with and a sense of what that continuity must have meant to any poet working within it.

In this book I have inevitably given an unfavourable impression of the courtly movement. The medieval courtly lyric in France or in England never achieved the range and subtlety which some Occitanian and Italian writers brought to it, and as we find it at the beginning of the sixteenth centry it is scarcely likely to impress anyone. For all that it is important to remember that there is nothing in the spirit of courtly love itself which inevitably leads to the creation of bad poetry. The best of the courtly poets have far more to offer than the kind of platitudinous laments which abound in the literature of medieval France. People often see nothing in the tradition except the hopeless love yearnings of feckless youths, the monotonous pursuit of love governed by a series of inflexible rules. This is unfortunate, for I think the great strength of the courtly movement lies precisely in its ability to deal with a wide range of emotions and desires, from the most carnal to the most sublime, from light-hearted game to high seriousness. There is a sophistication about the courtly world which can easily degenerate into mere posturing, but there is nothing in the convention which commands uniformity of sentiment or expression.

To illustrate this point about the flexibility of the courtly tradition I will look briefly at one of the *cansos* (chansons) of the troubadour Bernard de Ventadour, who flourished in the third quarter of the twelfth century. The poem corresponds on the surface to many people's idea of what courtly love is all about. Bernard begins:

    Chantars no pot gaire valer,
    si d'ins dal cor no mou lo chans;

and he goes on to say that the only worthwhile song is that
which derives from *fin' amors coraus*, a noble and truly felt kind
of love. Then he says:

> Per so es mos chantars cabaus
> qu'en joi d'amor ai et enten
> la boch' e.ls olhs e.l cor e.l sen.[6]

This acknowledged dependence of the poet's senses on the
power of love is a theme which survives unchanged into the
sixteenth century, while the insistence on nobility of heart can
be linked to the preoccupations of the *dolce stil novo* poets in Italy
and is a theme which is picked up again by Chaucer, probably
in direct imitation of Guinizelli, for the great invocation to
Venus at the beginning of book three of *Troilus and Criseyde*:

> O blisful light, of which the bemes clere
> Adorneth al the thridde heven faire!
> O sonnes lief, O Joves doughter deere,   [*beloved of the sun*
> Plesance of love, O goodly debonaire,   [*O most gracious*
> In gentil hertes ay redy to repaire!   [*dwell*

Bernard, in his *canso*, goes on to stress further his happy
dependence on the purity of his love and to attack those who
debase its name through their stupidity, vulgarity, or venality.
Only submission to the beloved and a life of a contented
harmony of interests is worthy of the name of love:

> En agradar et en voler
> es l'amors de dos fis amans.
> Nula res no i pot pro tener,
> si.lh voluntatz non es egaus.
> E cel es be fols naturaus
> que, de so que vol, la repren
> e.lh lauza so que no.lh es gen.[7]

This seems the traditional picture of the courtly lover's
obedience and subservience. We might think, from his apparent
complacency and unreflecting lack of independence, that he is
devoid of any vitality. Yet this is simply to be taken in by the
lowest common denominators of the tradition, for Bernard was

also the poet who wrote, in the *canso* beginning 'Can vei la lauzeta mover':

> I despair of women;
> never again shall I put my trust in them;
> and as I used to defend them
> so now shall I abandon them . . .
> for I know well that they are all the same.

There is a contradiction here only if we view the courtly tradition as monolithic. In reality one is simply dealing with two different states of mind, and the convention is quite broad enough to accommodate them both. It would be quite wrong to suggest that the first *canso* alone is truly courtly and the second simply a temporary aberration from the tedious norm.

If one looks a little more closely at the apparently bland formulations of the first *canso* it is evident that the whole game is given away in the sixth stanza of the poem, when Bernard says:

> Mout ai be mes mo bon esper,
> cant cela.m mostra bels semblans
> qu'eu plus dezir e volh vezer . . .[8]

Anyone alive to the way the courtly lyric functions will know exactly what is going on here. When your beloved encourages you, however indirectly, there is no better way to proceed than to glorify the virtues of pure love and allow events to take their course. Standing in the background the lover can let his case plead itself, without the necessity of indulging in unseemly techniques of persuasion. And it is clear, moreover, that the lover is not really off stage. He manages to derive the excellence of his song from the *fin' amors* within his heart, rather than boasting openly about his talents, but the point will be taken, hopefully, by whoever is listening. And in the concluding lines of the poem Bernard opens up the perspectives on what he expects to follow:

> Lo vers es fis e naturaus
> e bos celui qui be l'enten;
> e melher es, qui.l joi aten.
>
> Bernartz de Ventadorn l'enten,
> e.l di e.l fai, e.l joi n'aten![9]

Peter Dronke comments on the use of the word *joi* in the poetry

of the troubadours, claiming that 'it is less a particular feeling
than a quality of mind, an attitude to life and way of life . . . a
permanent disposition, which is both cause and effect of love,
and gives him who has it unlimited potentialities of virtù'.[10] I
think that so restrictively complex an interpretation might
possibly have amused a twelth-century practitioner of the art of
poetry. For the usefulness of a term like *joi*, and of so many
other courtly terms, is that it defies precise definition, and this
reliance on a deliberate ambiguity of vocabulary remains an
important feature of the love lyric well into the sixteenth
century. *Joi* can mean anything, and that is what protects the
courtly participants. There is nothing in Bernard's song which
suggests sensuality and only that. His poem is discreet and could
be turned, according to the demands of the situation, either in a
physical direction towards the eventual consummation of love,
or in a purely spiritual sense to sanctify the state of bliss shared
by the two concerned.

It is interesting to read the speech which Pausanias makes in
Plato's *Symposium*, for it throws some light on the way in which
love conventions operate. At one point (182 A) Pausanias
compares the Athenian love codes with those existing in other
places, and he says that whereas in Athens these codes are
sophisticated and complex, elsewhere, as in Elis and Boeotia,
there is only the straightforward question of regularising sexual
gratification. In such vulgar regions they have no skill in speech,
and so there is little point in bothering with the refined pleasures
of love talk, but in Athens matters are infinitely more subtle and
much harder to understand. The moral is clear: you cannot have
refined love without refined ways of talking about it, and of
course nothing is more refined than ambiguity. The distance
which separates the world of Pausanias from that of the courtly
tradition is not very great. Henri Chamard talks about the
courtly code ('ce code singulier') and its objectives in the
following terms, maintaining that 'si la récompense ne doit
jamais être sollicitée, elle est néanmoins toujours espérée; et c'est
un dogme de ce code singulier, qu'Amour finit toujours par
guerredoner au centuple ses loyaux serviteurs'.[11] And in the very
manner of his writing Chamard perpetuates the ambiguity of
the courtly tradition. He means to say that patient love service
should always be sexually rewarded, but he does not say so
obviously, and resorts to the old courtly term *guerredoner* (= 'to

reward'), a term which is deliberately ambiguous and which was still flourishing in the sixteenth century.

The courtly tradition developed a large number of these semantically ambiguous expressions, and it is important that one should be alive to the way in which they are being employed. For example, in the few lines from the *canso* of Bernard de Ventadour that I quoted, we find, besides the word *joi*, terms such as *voler* and *voluntatz*. In the poetry of Scève, almost four hundred years later, *vouloir* and *volonté* are used in exactly the same way, and they can convey anything from purely spiritual yearnings to the most physical desires, or, very often, a deliberately indeterminable mixture of both. One can seldom be sure of the exact meaning of the abstract terms which Scève employs and it is interesting therefore to look at the following lines from the *Délie* where, for once, the mask of ambiguity falls:

> Plus pour esbat, que non pour me douloir
> De tousjours estre en passions brulantes,
> Je contentois mon obstiné vouloir:
> Mais je sentis ses deux mains bataillantes,
> Qui s'opposoient aux miennes travaillantes,
> Pour mettre a fin leur honneste desir.
>
> [dizain 309]

A dubious tale indeed. But the reader can only be really sure of the sense of the first three lines when he sees what follows. The true nature of the poet's desire (*vouloir*) becomes clear only when the language breaks away from the world of abstraction which Scève's poetry so frequently inhabits and becomes unambiguously concrete. The first lines by themselves, though suggestive, do not establish the sense of the poem beyond doubt, for the reader is accustomed to Scève's use of phrases such as 'sainctz vouloirs' and 'ma volonté sainctement obstinée' elsewhere in the *Délie*, in contexts which preserve a deliberately ambiguous atmosphere.[12] Even here, where the rather sordid game is quite given away, the poet instinctively and perhaps a little hopefully refers to his burning passion as an 'honneste desir'. When reading a collection such as the *Délie* it is important to remember the long erotic tradition which lies behind it. From all earlier periods of French love poetry there are countless examples of the conscious use of ambiguous abstractions, sometimes for very serious purposes, sometimes for the sheer delight of being ambiguous.

A most amusing illustration of the suggestive power of these abstractions occurs in Chartier's *La Belle Dame sans mercy*, where we find the lover in possession of a vast repertoire of terms with which he attempts to break down the lady's notorious resistance:

> Je ne quier point de guerredon,
> Car le desservir m'est trop hault:
> Je demande grace en pur don
> Puis que mort ou mercy me fault.
> Donner le bien ou il deffault,
> C'est courtoisie raisonnable,
> Mais aux siens encores plus vault
> Qu'estre aux estranges amÿable.

[ll. 417 ff.]

This is indeed a virtuoso performance. The lover seeks no obvious 'reward', for he declares himself undeserving of any. He begs only for the gift of grace, for mercy, and for the universal *bien* without which death is the only refuge. Moreover, he argues, to grant all this is only to behave in a courtly manner, to be *amÿable*, and women should wish to be kind and attentive to those nearest them. The lady is fortunately alive to all this and replies in effect: 'I don't know what you mean by "bien", but you're certainly not getting any from me', and her immediate thoughts of womanly honour drive the lover into a frenzy of self-justification:

> Oncq homme mortel ne nasqui
> Ou pourroit neistre soubz les cieulx —
> Et n'est autre, fors vous — a qui
> Voustre honneur touche plus ou mieulx
> Qu' a moy . . .

[ll. 433 ff.]

Some critics maintain that the word *bien* in these contexts should always be translated in an obviously sexual sense, and that is, I think, an approach which strikes at the basis of everything the courtly movement stands for.

As a last example of the difficulties and potentialities which the courtly tradition presents in its terminology, I refer the reader to the use of the word *courtly* itself. If one looks at the *Grande dizionario della lingua italiana* (sub *cortese*), or the *Middle*

English Dictionary edited by H. Kurath (sub *courteis*), or the *Altfranzösisches Wörterbuch* of Tobler-Lommatzsch (sub *cortois*), the range of possible meanings is at once apparent and is fascinating to observe. The adjective *courtly* can in fact be applied to almost anything. Its rather dubious side appears very early on: Giacomo da Lentini, who died between 1246 and 1250, uses the phrase *alla cortese* in the sense of 'surreptitiously', while Pierre Bec translates the expression *far cortesia* as 'mener la vie élégante' with reference to one of the poems of Iacopone da Todi (1230–1306).[13] Interestingly enough, George Kay, in *The Penguin Book of Italian Verse*, translates the simple *cortesia* as 'nobleness' with reference to another of Iacopone's poems, which further stresses the semantic range involved. Oliver is called *curteis* in the *Song of Roland*, Christ is referred to as *Cortayse* (a substantive) in the Middle English alliterative poem *Cleanness*, while Beatrice addresses Virgil as 'anima cortese' in *Inferno*, II, 58. At the other end of the scale we find the month of February being called the least courtly of months in some French lines quoted in Tobler-Lommatzsch. Of course love too can be courtly. The expression *courtly love* is not a creation of modern criticism, as one still sometimes hears it said. It is true that the phrase *cortez' amors* is rare in Occitanian, occurring perhaps only once in the poetry of the troubadours, but *amore cortese* is common enough amongst the Italians. In the hands of a poet like Cino da Pistoia, the friend of Dante and Petrarch, 'fino Amor cortese' can sum up all that the writer considers best and noblest in the emotional aspirations of man. Petrarch too, though he never uses the phrase *courtly love* in the *Canzoniere*, is capable of expressing the noblest sentiments through the term *courtesy*. In the sonnet beginning 'Spirto felice che sì dolcemente', he says that when his beloved Laura died the sun fell from the sky and Love and *cortesia* departed from the world. But Petrarch, it should be noted, was also very much alive to the ambiguous possibilities of courtesy, and in a poem of reproach and persuasion to the same Laura, the sonnet beginning 'S'una fede amorosa, un cor non finto', we find Scève's 'honest desire' expressed through the familiar phrases 'oneste voglie' and 'desiar cortese'.

It is not the aim of this book to trace the ambiguity of terminology and attitudes in the lyric tradition from the age of the first troubadours through to the sixteenth century. Doubtless such a survey needs to be done in detail, but it would be a large undertaking. What I have tried to do is to establish the extent to which early sixteenth-century poetry in France relied on the medieval courtly inheritance, so that the truly innovative nature of the work of Ronsard and du Bellay can be seen in its proper perspective. The delight in ambiguity is only one aspect of a generally abstract approach to love which dominates the French courtly tradition and which makes the vast majority of the lyrics associated with it largely inaccessible to the modern reader. The courtly game in France had become an extremely tedious affair by the beginning of the sixteenth century, and I think the achievement of Ronsard and du Bellay in breaking with the traditions they inherited was just as significant as they themselves liked to pretend. It would be a mistake, therefore, to suggest, as some have done, that the Pléiade simply revived the flagging fortunes of the traditional courtly lyric. If one looks simply at the question of themes, this may well appear to be the case, but anyone who comes to the *Olive* after reading the love lyrics in a collection such as the *Jardin de Plaisance* (c. 1501) will see that the difference between the two worlds is not in fact one of degree, but of kind. It is often said that modern French poetry began with the Pléiade, and in this book I have tried to show how and why I believe this to be true.

1 'Petrarchism' and the love poetry of Clément Marot

It would be fair to say that the best poets of the fifteenth century in France were François Villon (1431–?), Charles d'Orléans (1394–1465), and Alain Chartier (1380/1390?–1430). This short list in itself goes some way to account for the fact that the continuity of the courtly tradition, which was unbroken all through the fifteenth century, frequently passes unobserved. For the best poets were dead or had vanished long before 1500 and the greatest poet of them all, François Villon, is not intimately associated with the courtly lyric in the minds of most readers. In many respects the fifteenth century in France appears like its counterpart in Italy, a 'secolo senza poesia',[1] for even if you add the name of Christine de Pisan (c. 1364 – c. 1430) to the above three, the total amount of good poetry written during the century cannot be said to be very large. Moreover, the direct influence of these poets on the writers of the sixteenth century seems equally small, and there is therefore a natural tendency to dismiss the fifteenth century in general as late medieval and to establish a major break at some point so that the Renaissance may conveniently be ushered in. Of course there is always 'influence' if you wish to find it. Clément Marot published an edition of Villon's work; while some 254 poems by Charles d'Orléans found their way anonymously into a collection entitled *La Chasse et le départ d'amours*, published in 1509, a collection with which Ronsard was probably acquainted; and the name, at least, of Chartier lived on, as Daniel Poirion points out: 'son nom sera un des rares qui parviendront au public du XVI⁶ siècle encore entouré de tout son prestige', while it is worth noting that Marguerite de Navarre actually quotes from Chartier's *Belle Dame sans mercy* in the *Heptaméron*.[2] In general, however, there is not much evidence of direct exchange between fifteenth-century and sixteenth-century poets, and critics have thus usually paid little attention to the question. However, it can be shown that there was considerable exchange of an indirect, untraceable nature, and the consequences of this are most interesting to observe.

Before we move on to discuss this, it would be useful to say
something more about the state of French poetry in the fifteenth
century. I have suggested that the poets listed above did not
exert much personal influence on the succeeding century partly
because they all belonged to the earlier part of the fifteenth
century, the later part producing no writer who would now be
regarded as major. But there is obviously more to it than that.
Villon, in particular, may well appear even now to have been
inimitable. He does not belong to any well-defined category.
He could write readily in the manner of the courtly lover when
it suited him, but this is never sustained. Look at the following
lines from the *Testament*:

> Se celle que jadis servoie
> De si bon cuer et loyaument,
> Dont tant de maulx et griefz j'avoie
> Et souffroie tant de torment,
> Se dit m'eust, au commencement,
> Sa voulenté (mais nennil, las!)
> J'eusse mis paine aucunement
> De moy retraire de ses las.

> [ll. 673 ff.]

The vocabulary is totally familiar: the protestations of loyal and
willing love-service, the pains and torment of love, all these are
expressed through the common denominators of the courtly
tradition, while the reference to the snares (*las*) in which the
poet has been caught finds a counterpart already in the Egyptian
love songs:

> I shall set aside my nets.
> But what can I tell my mother
> to whom I return every day
> when I am laden with catch?

> I did not set my traps today;
> love of you has thus entrapped me.[3]

But Villon only makes use of this kind of language in passing.
He is not really interested in the potentialities available within
the courtly tradition. It is not that he is attacking love which
makes his lines essentially uncourtly in context—indeed at times
he can sound exactly like Bernard de Ventadour:

> Amans je ne suyvray jamais:

Se jadis je fus de leur ranc,
Je desclare que n'en suis mais.

[ll. 718–20]

What is important is the fact that the poet is using the language
of courtly love in the same way as he used the slang of the
dicing tables, or the image of the hangman's noose (ll. 689 ff.).
He is willing to take his material from any source which comes
to hand in order to develop the theme of the rejected lover, and
the final effect is quite unlike anything we have been
considering so far.

Charles d'Orléans was inimitable for very different reasons.
He was a fine lyric poet, but, as Pound would have put it, 'out
of key with his time'. Guiraut Riquier (d. 1292?), popularly
thought of as the last of the troubadours, spent much of his life
searching the southern courts for a base from which to practise
the dying art of the Occitanian lyric. Charles, on the other
hand, was fortunate enough to have a ready-made poetic base in
the shape of the small court of Blois, and it was to Blois that he
returned in 1441 after the twenty-five years he spent in England
as a prisoner following his capture at the battle of Agincourt
(1415). But if Charles had a secure position from which to
compose, in many ways his poetry too stands at the end of a
tradition, though doubtless he was less conscious of the fact that
Guiraut Riquier had been. It is curious to reflect that Villon
once stayed at Blois and that he composed a ballade in the series
'Je meurs de seuf [soif] auprés de la fontaine' as his contribution
to the so-called *Concours de Blois* of *c*. 1458–60. For one often has
the impression that the world of the small courts was a very
closed one. Indeed Daniel Poirion considers the existence of
centres like Blois as having been vital to the preservation of the
old aristocratic lyric tradition at a time when it was seriously
threatened by the growing influence of 'bourgeois rhetoric'.
Poirion points out that the fifteenth century in France witnessed
an expansion in the role being played by civil servants who had
received a legal, rather than a clerical, training, and he
comments: 'La rhétorique des légistes, la rhétorique laïque . . .
menace le lyrisme non seulement de son vocabulaire technique
. . . mais aussi de sa sécheresse.'[4] The existence of the small
courts exerted a beneficial influence against the dominant trend,
a trend which Poirion none the less sees as leading inexorably to

the poetry of the Grands Rhétoriqueurs ('the great literary industry of Burgundy'): 'Cette diffusion du lyrisme orléanais, au moment même où la grande industrie littéraire de Bourgogne tend à submerger la France, permettra aux valeurs et aux goûts qu'on peut appeler courtois de subsister jusqu'au XVIe siècle, à côté des tendances nouvelles de la poésie rhétorique et satirique.' This link between the poetry of the early sixteenth century and the courtly world often passes unnoticed and this is largely due to the anonymous, and generally unremarkable, quality of most late fifteenth-century verse. But if the influence is difficult to trace, it is certainly present none the less: 'Nombreux sont les poèmes anonymes de la fin du siècle qui attestent la survivance des motifs poétiques mis à la mode par le duc d'Orléans et ses amis.'[5]

What I think is strictly inimitable about the poetry of Charles is his handling of the medieval abstract/allegorical tradition. Many poets in the early sixteenth century continued to use the debris of that tradition, but Charles is the last major poet to exploit its resources successfully as a means of communicating and analysing the experience of love. Perhaps it is simply the atmosphere of the court at Blois, but there is something extremely refined about his poetry, and in the relationships between his personified figures there is a delightful intimacy, a sense of a completely natural family world that I think was never recaptured by any later lyric poet. The following lines provide a good illustration of the point:

> Quant je suis couschié en mon lit,
> Je ne puis en paix reposer;
> Car toute la nuit mon cueur lit
> Ou rommant de Plaisant Penser,
> Et me prie de l'escouter;
> Si ne l'ose desobeir
> Pour doubte de le courroucer:
> Ainsi je laisse le dormir.[6]

Charles is dealing entirely with an abstract world, but the impression he conveys is one of easy familiarity and the 'Romance of Pleasant Thoughts' which, we learn, contains nothing but the deeds of his beloved, seems an eminently suitable bedside book in the context of the poem. The situation is rather different if we look at an analagous dizain from Scève's *Délie*:

Tout le repos, ô nuict, que tu me doibs,
Avec le temps mon penser le devore:
Et l'Horologe est compter sur mes doigtz
Depuis le soir jusqu'a la blanche Aurore.
    Et sans du jour m'appercevoir encore,
Je me pers tout en si doulce pensée,
Que du veiller l'Ame non offensée,
Ne souffre au Corps sentir celle douleur
De vain espoir tousjours recompensée
Tant que ce Monde aura forme, & couleur.

[dizain 232]

Once again the poet lies awake at night, troubled, but at the same time indulging in his thoughts. Though love is nowhere mentioned it is clear that the impulse towards thought derives from that source, and Scève has already described its effects in numerous other poems in the *Délie*. It is interesting to note that the argument of dizain 232 is carried by a number of abstractions such as *penser*, *doulce pensée*, *Ame*, *Corps*, *vain espoir*, abstractions which in the hands of Charles d'Orléans would have been securely placed within the allegorical family, but which Scève uses in a far less personalized way. Scève's abstractions are vaguely in touch with each other, it is true, for *Ame* is seen to be protecting *Corps* on a concrete, physical level, but this kind of relationship is never sustained. Look, for example, at Scève's handling of *doulce pensée*. This figure is a creation of the Middle Ages and it has a clear emotional function to fulfil, as the lover in the *Roman de la Rose* finds out:

Li premiers biens qui solaz face
Ceus que li laz d'Amors enlace,
C'est Douz Pensers, qui lor recorde
Ce ou Esperance s'acorde.
Quant li amanz plaint e sospire,
E est en duel e en martire,
Douz Pensers vient a chief de piece,
Qui l'ire e la dolor despiece,
E a l'amant en son venir
Fait de la joie sovenir
Que Esperance li promet.[7]

When the lover is suffering from his attachment, *Douz Pensers* sets before him the image of his beloved and the process of memory gladdens his heart again:

Si li plaist mout quant il li membre
De la biauté de chascun membre.

[ll. 2659–60]

But for Scève the figure of *doulce pensée* has become an almost
total abstraction. Behind it lies the whole emotional world of
the *Roman de la Rose*, and the role which it plays in Scève's poem
is exactly the role for which it was originally designed, but the
relationship with the lover/poet is no longer an intimate one.
The use of the verb *se perdre* and the adverb *si* (l. 6) shows that
one of the two fundamental levels of allegory has been lost, and
the retreat of the poet into his thoughts can only be appreciated
on an abstract level, with no real correspondence on the level of
the physical. In the case of the noun *penser* in l. 2 the effect is
similar, for there is no attempt to make the verb *dévorer* appear
very graphic in context. This is characteristic of Scève's
handling of abstractions. One often feels that he has a desire to
hold them at arm's length and that their role is simply that of a
conventional emotional shorthand. There is nothing about the
abstract/allegorical tradition which makes it inevitably dull and
lifeless for the modern reader—it is entirely a matter of
presentation. In the case of Scève one often wishes he could
have found an alternative method of conveying his argument,
but in the ballade by Charles that I quoted the whole strength of
the poem derives from the free and easy manner in which the
abstract figures are portrayed. Charles conveys the feelings of
pleasure, fear, and, in the final stanza of the ballade, sheer
exhaustion which beset the lover in a way that is totally
convincing in its own terms. And when the poet concludes that
he is unable to control his heart because he is so much in love,
this simple emotional truth is expressed quite naturally in terms
of the devotion of *cueur* to *Amour* on an intimate, totally
personalised level:

Amour, je ne puis gouverner
Mon cueur; car tant vous veult servir
Qu'il ne scet jour ne nuit cesser:
Ainsi je laisse le dormir.

The strengths of the Scève dizain lie in very different areas. One
notes, for example, the image of the clock in l. 3: 'Et l'Horologe
est compter sur mes doigtz' ('And the clock is counted on my
fingers'), or the way in which the poem suddenly opens out at

the end after the claustrophobia of the preceeding lines so that the poet can generalise the particular experience he has been describing.

I would like to show that this brief comparison between Scève and Charles d'Orléans has a general validity. The successful analysis and communication of love through the abstract/allegorical system is something one rarely finds after Charles, and, though the vocabulary of the system remained in use as an essential element of the courtly tradition, love poetry in France tended to be irredeemably abstract in its attitudes until the advent of the Pléiade. I shall leave further demonstration of this point until later chapters, and I turn now to an examination of the state of French poetry around the year 1500. For our purposes the *Jardin de Plaisance et Fleur de Rhétorique* is an ideal starting point. This work is an immensely interesting collection of poetry and it is a pity that the only available edition is the facsimile reproduction of the original Paris edition of *c.* 1501, made for the Société des Anciens Textes Français in 1910. The text is not very easy for the general reader to follow, though there is much practical assistance to be gained from the volume of introductory material and notes which E. Droz and A. Piaget added in 1925. The work extends over more than five hundred pages and contains over seven hundred items. There are eight known editions of the *Jardin*, of which the first is the only complete one. The last was published in 1527, and there is a Lyon edition around 1525. As S. Cigada points out in his entry on the *Jardin* for the *Dictionnaire des lettres françaises* (*Le Moyen Age*), the poems represented constitute 'une véritable synthèse de toute la poésie courtoise depuis Guillaume de Machaut jusqu'aux "grands rhétoriqueurs"', and the collection in fact provides a clear demonstration of Daniel Poirion's thesis concerning the survival of the old courtly tradition in the early sixteenth century. Virtually every poem in the *Jardin* is given without indication of author, though Droz and Piaget managed to establish the identity in a fair number of cases. Guillaume de Machaut, one of the most important figures in the fourteenth century, both as poet and as musician, is represented by six ballades and two rondeaux. Eustache Deschamps (*c.* 1346 – *c.* 1406), the most important of Machaut's poetic disciples, is represented by six ballades too, while a number of ballades by Villon are included, including the 'Ballade de la Grosse

Margot'. There are seven rondeaux by Charles d'Orléans and three poems by Alain Chartier, one of them extremely long, the *Débat des deux fortunés d'amours*. The rhétoriqueur tradition is well represented, though it is by no means as overwhelming as one might have expected at this period. Molinet, Meschinot, Cretin, and Chastelain are all included.

The dominant impression which the *Jardin* creates is one of a delightfully unselfconscious diffuseness. The various ballades and rondeaux which form the bulk of the collection are vaguely understood to have been recited in the pleasure garden which gives its name to the work, that *locus amoenus* which, as Curtius suggests, 'from the Empire to the sixteenth century . . . forms the principal motif of all nature description'.[8] But apart from this there is a complete lack of any unifying theme. In addition to the short poems in fixed forms there are a number of poems which are quite long, including the débat by Chartier already mentioned. There is a *Débat de l'homme marié et de l'homme non marié* and a *Débat du Cœur et de l'Œil*, while at one point (fo. cciii v.) the rubric relates 'Comment l'amant yssant du jardin de plaisance entra en la forest cuydant avoir plus de joye, et il entra en tristesse en plusieurs façons', which is the prelude to a poem some five thousand lines in length. The first pages of the *Jardin*, on the other hand, are given over to an Art of Poetry, which, being itself written in verse, is extraordinarily difficult to follow and not particularly illuminating at that. Droz and Piaget considered that this Art of Poetry had been written during the reign of Louis XI (1461–83). Alain Chartier is cited by the author as 'entier grand maistre' (fo. v), a position which he still occupies in Pierre Fabri's *Le Grand et Vrai Art de pleine rhétorique*, a poetic treatise published in 1521. The most interesting part of the Art of Poetry in the *Jardin* is the ninth chapter, in which the author gives examples of various verse forms, including a two-syllable and a one-syllable rondeau. The main verse forms are all represented, rondeau, virelai, ballade, and so on, forms with eminently respectable traditions behind them, but which were suddenly to be classed as 'episseries' by du Bellay, and as 'vieille quinquaille roüillée' by Jacques Tahureau. Within a remarkably short time the sonnet was to establish itself as *the* medium for serious love poetry, and the world of the ballade and the rondeau, which appears unshakeable in the *Jardin*, had in reality very little life ahead in sixteenth-century France. For L. Forster the introduction of the sonnet is important not only from the point of view of form: it is symptomatic of a basic change in inspiration, and he expresses the relationship in the following way: 'In all countries outside Italy the acclimatisation of petrarchism does not succeed until the appropriate verse form is also acclimatised, in which petrarchistic diction can be adequately expressed.'9 What is beyond doubt is that the whole substance of the love poetry in the *Jardin*, and not just its verse forms, is made to seem quite outmoded by the advent of the Pléiade.

This fact is all the more interesting when one considers how little French poetry seems to have changed between the time of Machaut (*c.* 1300–77) and the date of the *Jardin*. Of course a sixteenth-century reader may well have thought differently, but I can find no satisfactory stylistic criteria for differentiating between the various chronological levels in the collection. There is considerable variety in the poetry of the *Jardin*, but the general quality is timeless. Look at the following lines, for example, from a ballade by Machaut which appears at fo. lxv:

> Or ay perdu tout bien, toute doulçour,
> Joye, soulas, jeux, ris, esbatement,
> Mon doulx espoir, mon desir, mon labour,
> Par bien servir et aymer loyaument.

This is a typical lover's complaint in the grand manner, the courtly tradition operating entirely from its common denominators, to a modern reader quite lifeless and banal. But, as the rubric at fo. lx points out, there are a great many different kinds of ballade and rondeau in the collection, some to the glory of women, others to their everlasting dishonour. If one tires of the endless succession of courtly platitudes there are always poems such as the *Balade des abus des femmes*, which could scarcely be further from the spirit of courtly love, however defined:

> Puis que femmes furent bonnes galoises,
> Puis qu'a force plumerent leurs visaiges,
> Puis qu'ilz [*sic*] mirent en leurs chaperons boises,
> Puis qu'ilz firent aux tetins fenestrages
> Puis qu'en chançons par trop fut leur couraiges . . .

> [fo. lxiiii]

And so it goes on, the whole ballade formed around a succession

of complaints against women, with over thirty lines introduced
by 'Puis que', followed by a specific charge. This is standard
medieval anti-feminism, what C. S. Lewis once called 'one of
the ugliest tendencies in medieval thought', though it can also
be extremely amusing, as any reader of Chaucer will agree. The
world of this ballade is that of the Wife of Bath; women always
wish to interfere in things which do not concern them, they
always want money and fine clothes, to be seen at fairs and to
go on pilgrimages; they parade their sexuality, they even, as the
ballade tells us, wish to sleep 'au dextre du lict'. After this series
of complaints it is perhaps refreshing to read the rondeau which
follows, for, if it is a long way from the world of courtly
sophistication, it shows at least an element of good sense behind
the traditional attack on women's love of dressing up:

> Ce me semblent choses perdues
> De vestir femmes richement;
> Car qui en veult esbatement,
> Avoir on les demande nues.

> [fo. lxiiii v.]

✗ If, for our present purposes, we are bound to concentrate on
the more courtly aspects of the *Jardin*, it is worth remembering
that sixteenth-century readers do not seem to have been very
worried about the juxtaposition of widely different sorts of
material. The contrast between courtly decorum and traditional
obscenity, between the praise of women and the vulgar abuse
of women, seems to have been accepted quite naturally.
Apparently the same people read both kinds of poetry, and
though this is what common sense tells one is likely in any case,
the notion of two kinds of audience and two kinds of medieval
mind is one that dies hard. Let it be said once again that it is not
the presence or absence of sexuality which makes a poem
courtly or not courtly; everything depends on the treatment in
the particular case. Against the unsophisticated treatment of the
rondeau quoted above, we can set the following exquisitely
erotic lines from Bernard de Ventadour's *canso* beginning 'Lo
gens tems de pascor':

> Las! e viure que.m val,
> s'eu no vei a jornal
> mo fi joi natural
> en leih, sotz fenestral,

cors blanc tot atretal
com la neus a nadal,
si c'amdui cominal
mesurem s'em egal?[10]

Moshé Lazar, in his edition of the love songs of Bernard, points out how earlier critics have refused to see the erotic tone that is so clearly expressed here and it is partly because of such critical resistance that courtly love has achieved its curiously etiolated reputation. Denys Page has similarly shown how critics can build the most wildly unhistorical theories around the poetry of Sappho, simply because they cannot accept that she could have written of women in erotic terms.[11] As I have suggested, it is vital that one should be alive to the nuances of the courtly tradition, that one should be prepared for the great emotional range of which it is capable. The love which is refined and the love which requires sexual fulfilment can only be separated artificially, even when, as is sometimes the case, the desire for such separation becomes the stimulus to the creation of the poem itself.

The fact that many of the poems in the *Jardin* bear witness to the survival of the courtly tradition is of some importance for the literary historian. For it is the debris of that tradition which critics have tended to confuse with what they identify as a growing Italian influence on the French lyric and it is to this question that I now turn. Until recently more or less general agreement existed amongst critics with regard to the dating of Italian influence on sixteenth-century French poetry. There was inevitable disagreement about which particular poet should be regarded as the 'first' Petrarchist in France and there was disagreement too about the exact form of Petrarchism involved—whether, that is, French poets were following Petrarch himself or his fifteenth-century Italian imitators—but most critics subscribed to the view that Italian influence began to exert itself in France during the 1530s, and the exile of Marot in Ferrara (1535–36) was generally considered to be of significance in this respect.[12] In the course of his valuable work on Marot, however, C. A. Mayer has proposed a new chronology, claiming that: 'It is precisely in his [Marot's] early poems, composed in the main before 1527, that Petrarchist inspiration is most evident'.[13] According to this thesis, then, Petrarchism is a phenomenon dating from at least the 1520s rather than the 1530s, and indeed the exile in Ferrara, far from marking the start of a movement, would, Mayer maintains, have marked the end of one. Marot would have discovered in Italy that the form of Petrarchism he had been following—the 'préciosité mignarde' of poets such as Serafino, Tebaldeo and so on—was now out of fashion, having been superseded by the 'pétrarquisme épuré' of the Bembist school.[14] He would thus have been led to abandon Petrarchism as a source of inspiration. The claim is an interesting one, but I think it can be shown that it is almost entirely without foundation and that a careful reading of a collection such as the *Jardin* will demonstrate the point easily enough.

If Marot is to be regarded as an innovator, a very early French Petrarchist, what are the criteria for deciding thus in his favour? Mayer writes: 'It is in the *rondeaux* [of Marot] that are to be found all the most characteristic devices of Petrarchist poetry, the antitheses, the fire and water, heat and ice images, the conceits of the exchange of hearts, the heart and the body, nature sympathizing with the lover's suffering, the wounds inflicted by the cruel lady, and the unhappy lover cherishing his suffering.'[15] Mayer's appeal, therefore, is to the cumulative evidence of recurring themes and devices, but the necessary qualification is that many of these themes and devices were widespread in French poetry before Marot and may simply witness to a common inheritance. Mayer's method of demonstrating Petrarchan influence is illustrated by his remark on Marot's *Rondeau par contradictions*: 'l'usage des antithèses pour exprimer la force de l'amour est un des *concetti* pétrarquistes les plus fréquents ... L'inspiration pétrarquiste est donc ici évidente.'[16] While the first part of this statement is undeniably true, the second is by no means the only possible conclusion. The device of the antithesis is very commonly used in love poetry generally, and to infer a Petrarchan influence solely on the basis of a shared device may well be misleading. Marot's poem reads as follows:

> En esperant, espoir me desespere
> Tant que la mort m'est vie tres prospere;
> Me tourmentant de ce qui me contente,
> Me contentant de ce qui me tourmente
> Pour la douleur du soulas que j'espere.

Amour hayneuse en aigreur me tempere;
Puis temperance aspre comme Vipere
Me refroidist soubz chaleur vehemente
  En esperant.
L'enfant aussi, qui surmonte le pere,
Bande ses yeulx pour veoir mon impropere;
De moy s'enfuyt & jamais ne s'absente,
Mais, sans bouger, va en obscure sente
Cacher mon dueil affin que mieulx appere
  En esperant.[17]

Mayer quotes four Italian poems, two by Petrarch and two by Chariteo, in connection with this rondeau, yet textual similarities between the French and Italian poems are striking only if we are eager to find them. All that is obviously shared is the antithetical manner, and this may as easily be illustrated by reference to Marot's French predecessors as to his Italian ones. Here is one of the Chariteo sonnets cited by Mayer:

Poi che saper volete in quale stato,
  Madonna, Amor servendo, io mi ritrovo,
  Odite il mal meraviglioso & novo,
  Che sempre mi procura il duro fato.
Per l'aere vo volando, & son portato
  Da tempestosi venti, & non mi movo;
  Et caldo & freddo ogn' hora inseme provo,
  E spero da speranza abbandonato.
D'un monte chiaro & pien di bianca neve
  Esce la fiamma ardente che mi strugge,
  E tremo ove m'accende il gran desio.
Veggio Amor che si mostra hor grave, hor lieve,
  Hor mi segue correndo, & hor mi fugge:
  Quest' è 'l morire, & questo è 'l viver mio.
                    [*Le rime*, Naples, 1892, sonnet 18][18]

The following extract, on the other hand, from a poem which appears in the *Jardin*, seems at least as close to the Marot text in tone and technique:

Assouvy suis, mais, sans cesser, desire,
Je me souhetz et ne me peut suffire,
Las je languys et suis content d'amours,
Je suis bien seur et me doubte tousjours,
A vostre advis dois je plourer ou rire?

> J'ay tous plaisirs et si viz en martire,
> Je suis sain et voys querant le mire . . .[19]

It is perhaps worth pointing out, moreover, that this piece, like
the Marot poem, is a rondeau and that both are thus linked by
their form to a well-defined French poetic tradition, whereas
the Italian poems quoted by Mayer are all sonnets. In such
conditions, where there are no obvious reasons to prefer an
Italian source to a French one, it seems necessary to approach the
question of 'Petrarchan' influence with some caution. Not that I
believe the Marot poem to be in any direct sense derived from
the poem in the *Jardin*, any more than I think it derives from the
four Italian poems, only that here is an illustration of the
existence of a particular device in both French and Italian poetry
and that therefore there is no reason to stress Italian examples at
the expense of French ones in attempting to define the context
of this rondeau. As Marcel Françon wrote (in 1943): 'Je vois
dans ce rondeau [the *Rondeau par contradictions*] la marque de la
tradition   médiévale   française   plus   que   de   la   tradition
pétrarquiste.'[20] The ambiguities in the world of love had long
been expressed through the device of the antithesis, whether in
Italy or in France, and there seems no point in looking for
specific sources. There are, however, a number of critics who
proceed on the assumption that particular Italian sources can in
fact be found for a wide range of poems like the Marot rondeau
and who see the critic's primary task as the identification of
those sources. This approach raises problems that are simply
theoretical. Thus Mayer writes: 'Alors qu'il est aisé de voir que
Marot a emprunté à la poésie pétrarquiste des thèmes et des
concetti célèbres, il est infiniment plus difficile d'en trouver les
sources précises.' M. White comments on a poem by Jean
Picart: 'The phraseology can easily be traced to Serafino, but its
precise origin is difficult to establish.' E. Parturier writes of
Maurice Scève: 'J'ai bien souvent, au cours de mes lectures, cru
tenir une source de la *Délie*, et découvert ensuite qu'il y en avait
d'autres semblables.'[21] The need to cite four Italian poems to
'account for' so simple a poem as the *Rondeau par contradictions* is
in itself suggestive. It is a preoccupation with the supposed
importance of Italian influence on French poetry which leads to
the collection of as many Italian poems as are required to cover
the essentially banal range of images in the Marot poem. There

is no consideration of the possibility that one may be dealing with themes and devices that had long been common property in Marot's time.

One may pass on to consider some of the other criteria of Petrarchism suggested by Mayer. For the theme of the unhappy lover cherishing his suffering he refers to Tebaldeo in particular, while commenting that the idea 'est fréquente dans la poésie pétrarquiste'.[22] This theme also appears in France before Marot, as illustrated in another poem from the *Jardin*:

> Si je seuffre belle pour vostre amour
> Tresdoulcement et de bon cueur l'endure;
> Car tant me plaist l'amoureuse poincture
> Qu'amours me fait en vous servant souffrir
> Que ma douleur me rend ung grant plaisir . . .
>
> [fo. cxxiii]

Or compare the line:

> Hellas, le mal me plaist que me faictes sentir . . .
>
> [fo. cxxxiii v.]

It is a theme which one finds too in many of the poems of Alain Chartier, in the *Débat des deux fortunés d'amours*, for example, at l. 85, or at l. 790 ('Leur mal leur plaist, puis de leur joye pleurent'). The theme of the wounds inflicted by the cruel lady is another frequent one in earlier French poetry, and there seems no good reason to invoke Petrarchan influence to account for such lines as:

> Las, elle m'a navré de grand vigueur,
> Non d'ung cousteau, ne par haine ou rigueur,
> Mais d'ung baiser de sa bouche vermeille . . .
>
> [Marot, *Œuvres Diverses*, No. 49]

One may compare the following lines:

> Hellas, ma dame, qu'est ce la?
> Vostre doulx oeil qui me navra . . .
>
> [*Jardin*, fo. lxix v.]

While a slight variation may be seen in the lines from a ballade in Baudet Herenc's *Le Doctrinal de la Seconde Rhétorique* of 1432:

> Son doulx regard, qui tant est gent archier,
> De hault plaisir la fleche a volu traire
> Dedens mon cueur, sans le vouloir blechier . . .[23]

Which may in turn be compared with the opening of one of Marot's rondeaux:

> Avant mes jours mort me fault encourir
> Par ung regard dont m'as voulu ferir . . .
>
> [*Œuvres Diverses*, No. 11]

With reference to the conceit of the exchange of hearts, Mayer seeks to demonstrate the direct influence of Bembo on one of Marot's poems from the *Œuvres Diverses*. If Bembo's influence could be shown to have operated in France at so early a point in the sixteenth century, it might well be considered significant, but the evidence for such influence is meagre. Once again one notes the lack of any strong stylistic or linguistic similarities between the French and Italian poems to which Mayer refers. Bembo's lines read as follows:

> Ma quei, come 'l movesse un bel desire
> di non star con altrui del regno a parte,
> o fosse 'l ciel che lo scorgesse in parte
> ov'altro signor mai non devea gire,
> là, onde mosse il mio, lieto sen' venne
> così cangiaro albergo, e da quell' ora
> meco 'l cor vostro e 'l mio con voi dimora.[24]

Marot's poem is far removed from the lofty tone of Bembo, and his reference to an exchange of hearts is expressed conversationally in a way that is reminiscent of many earlier French poems; here are the relevant lines:

> Si tu le veulx, metz le [= ce cueur] soubz ta commande!
> Si tu le prendz, las, je te recommande
> Le triste Corps! ne le laisse sans Cueur!
> Mais loges y le tien, qui est vainqueur
> De l'humble Serf qui son vouloir te mande
>   Tant seullement.
>
> [*Œuvres Diverses*, No. 52]

One may compare the lines from the *Jardin*:

> Rendez moy le cueur qui fut mien
> Ou le traictiez plus doulcement . . .
>
> [fo. cxxi]

or:

> Je m'en vois et mon cueur demeure . . .
>
> [fo. lxxxviii v.]

or:

> A ce coup n'est mon cueur plus mien,
> Ne je n'y vueil avoir plus rien
> Car la belle le m'a tolu . . .

> [fo. lxxxviii v.]

It may be objected that Marot is calling for an exchange of
hearts, whereas the above examples from the *Jardin* refer to a
strictly unilateral condition, but one is tempted to conclude, in
the absence of any other examples of Bembo's 'influence', that
the dissimilarity in tone between the Bembo and Marot poems is
of greater significance than any superficial identity of theme.
Moreover, the conception of reciprocity is not in any sense
foreign to the French poetic tradition, as the following lines
from the *Jardin* illustrate:

> Car vraiement je suis bien seure
> Que noz deux cueurs s'entraimeront,
> Puis qu'en moy le sien fait demeure
> Tous d'ung vouloir pareil seront . . .

> [fo. lxxxix]

In any case, there is a long European tradition dealing in such
themes as the migrating heart, the stolen heart, exchanges of one
kind or another, separations of heart and body or soul and body,
and so on. These themes had long been linked in poetry of many
kinds, and there seems little reason to suppose a direct
connection between two such different poets as Marot and
Bembo in these circumstances. Mayer himself points out that the
conceit of the exchange of hearts may be found in French poetry
as early as Chrétien de Troyes (fl. 1160–90), while Robert
Breton, in a letter to Sainte-Marthe around 1537, reminds one
of the ancient tradition of the exchange of souls between lovers,
a tradition to which the less Platonic, more courtly, theme of
the exchange of hearts belongs: 'Scitum est n. illud Catonis, &
tibi opinor minime inauditum, animum amantis in alterius
corpore vivere.'[25] And C. Ruutz-Rees reminds one of the health
of the old body and soul debate in the early Renaissance,
referring to 'that famous mediaeval *Débat du corps et de l'âme*,
whose composition dates back at least to the early twelfth
century, and the endurance of whose popularity was proved by
its publication in the early sixteenth'.[26]
The problems surrounding the use of the term Petrarchism

derive, then, from the fact that many of the themes and devices adduced as Petrarchan have a well-assimilated position in French poetry at least as early as the beginning of the sixteenth century. P. M. Smith, in her book on Marot, highlights the logical difficulties involved, though without accepting what seem to be the obvious conclusions. She follows Mayer closely, sometimes textually, in her discussion of Petrarchism, but refers at one point to 'the features common to fifteenth-century French lyricism and to Petrarchism independently of each other and through their common origin in the work of the *trouvères*'. This seems close to the heart of the matter, but she goes on to offer her observation as 'one of the reasons why the Petrarchist sources of some of the *rondeaux* [of Marot] have for so long escaped notice and identification', though at the same time she recognises that 'in effect, this new source of inspiration did not greatly alter the treatment of an identical theme in the two genres'.[27] The problem is clear: how can one hope to dissociate foreign from native elements when there are no outstanding differences between the two? And yet, if one wishes to demonstrate positive influence, the establishment of parallels between, for example, Marot and an Italian poet must be supported by adequate criteria for distinguishing between what was already in the native tradition and what may plausibly have been borrowed into it—the mere establishment of parallels without further reference proves very little.

Some further themes which are current in discussions of Petrarchism may be considered briefly here. M. White has found what she terms 'most probably the earliest example in the sixteenth century' of the ice and fire antithesis in a poem by Jean Picart, who died before 1525.[28] This is a most interesting discovery, but one wonders whether the device was as new to the French tradition as M. White suggests. She writes: 'French versifiers at the end of the fifteenth century . . . had always burned with the flame of love, but the antithesis of ice and fire is not employed at all.' However, it would have been surprising, perhaps, had the ice and fire antithesis totally failed to find a place in the general antithetical tradition before the time of Jean Picart. One thinks in this context of Charles d' Orléans. Here is the opening of one of his ballades, written *c.* 1451:

Je meurs de soif en couste la fontaine;
Tremblant de froid ou feu des amoureux;[29]

The imagery in both lines was taken up again by the
contributors to the *Concours de Blois* (c. 1458–60). Here is the
opening of Villon's contribution:

> Je meurs de seuf auprés de la fontaine;
> Chault comme feu, et tremble dent a dent;
> En mon pays, suis en terre loingtaine;
> Lez ung brasier, frissonne tout ardent;[30]

The *Jardin* too has a lover: 'Froit comme glace et chault
comme charbon . . . ' (fo. cxliii), while Chartier's *Débat des deux
fortunés d'amours* is also quite at home in the world of the icy fire.
In the course of a long oxymoronic passage on the effects of love
we find the following lines:

> Hayneuse paix et guerre enamouree,
> Eur envïeux,
> Coursant esbat, jeu melencolïeux,
> Repos penible et tourment gracïeux,
> Plaisant ennuy et plaisir ennuyeux,
> Fiel emmielé,
> Chaude friçon, eaue ardant, feu gelé . . .
>
> [ll. 1086–92]

The obvious difference between these examples and the poem
by Jean Picart is that the antithesis in the latter is more fully
developed and instead of the lover experiencing the extremes
within himself it is the lady who remains cold as ice while the
lover continually burns with love:

> Plus chault que feu ne que metail en fonte
> Est mon las cueur, qu'amour contrainct et dompte
> A pourchasser d'une dame la grace,
> Toute gelee, et qui en froideur passe
> Vent, neige et gresle au temps que bise monte.

Whether these differences are significant or not is difficult to say
and I shall return to the point later.

The theme of the sweet breath of the lady is one which Marot
employs in the following lines:

> Mais le mien cueur adonc plus elle enflamme,
> Car son alaine odorant plus que basme
> Souffloit le feu qu'Amour m'a preparé
> En la baisant.
>
> [*Œuvres Diverses*, No. 55]

Mayer suggests that Petrarchan influence may be detected here, but one notes that the language is very close to that of the *Roman de la Rose*, of which Marot himself published an edition in 1527:

> E quant dou baisier me recors,
> Qui me mist une odor ou cors
> Assez plus douce que de basme,
> Par un poi que je ne me pasme,
> Qu'encor ai je ou cuer enclose
> La douce savor de la rose . . .

[ll. 3773–8]

The *Jardin* provides examples of a number of other relevant themes in this context. One finds reference to the lover's eyes as the cause of his downfall: 'Hellas! mes yeulx, mon cueur avez trahy . . .' [fo. cix v.], one finds the theme of the hunted stag identified with the lover (fo. cxcix v.), and one finds throughout the work poems which stress the beauty and virtue of the lady or the living death which the lover endures. Elsewhere one finds a fifteenth-century example of the theme of the hard-hearted woman compared to a diamond: 'O dame au cueur plus dur que fin diament . . .'[31]

A predisposition towards Petrarchan explanations naturally has an effect on one's assessment of particular details, but once again caution is called for. Thus Mayer makes the following comment on Marot's use of the word *enamouré* in the line 'Dont se mouroit le corps enamouré': 'Par l'usage de cet italianisme', he writes, 'Marot semble avouer son imitation de la poésie d'amour italienne.'[32] A glance at Godefroy or Huguet's dictionaries, however, reveals that the word had long been in use in France in contexts very similar to that of the Marot poem. A similar example of italianising may be seen in connection with Scève's use of the noun *Montgibel* in dizain 111 of the *Délie*:

> Lors tu verroys, tout autour a la ronde,
> De mes souspirs le Montgibel fumer.

E. Parturier notes that this proper noun is 'emprunté à Pétrarque', while I. D. McFarlane remarks that it is 'Petrarch's word for Etna'. But the context of the word is much wider than either critic suggests, since, as E. Langlois points out: 'C'est le nom que porte l'Etna au moyen âge dans de nombreux textes.'[33] This tendency to restrict the scope of critical comment, to emphasise the Italian tradition at the expense of possible parallels in the French tradition, is evident too in remarks such as those of E. Parturier on dizain 71 of the *Délie*, which is in the form of a débat: 'Ce genre de dialogue', he writes in his note on the poem, 'est très fréquent chez les Pétrarquisants.' One also finds examples in the *Jardin*, one of which is the famous *Débat du Cuer et du Corps de Villon* (fo. cviii).

Of course it is not suggested that Italian literature was totally unknown in early sixteenth-century France. The existence of translations, if nothing else, proves otherwise. Jean Marot's poem, 'S'il est ainsi que ce corps t'abandonne', is a translation of Serafino, and E. M. Rutson comments on two other poems of Jean Marot from before 1518 which she also derives from Serafino. M. White further quotes two rondeaux, published before 1527, which she considers 'almost literal translations of poems by Serafino'.[34] The existence of such translations—and doubtless more will be found—should, however, be viewed in the proper perspective. None of them to date shows much evidence of a departure from the traditional forms and techniques common in French poetry of the time, as the text of the following poem by Jean Marot illustrates:

> S'il est ainsi que ce corps t'abandonne,
> Amour commande & la raison ordonne
> Que je te laisse en gaige de ma foy
> Le cueur ja tien, car par honneste loy
> Aulcun ne doibt reprendre ce qu'il donne.
>   Ne croy jamais qu'aillieurs il s'abandonne!
> Plus tost la mort (sans que Dieu luy pardonne)
> Le puisse prendre & meurtrir devant toy
>   S'il est ainsi.
>
> Si Faulx rapport qui les amantz blasonne
> Te vient disant que j'ayme aultre personne,
> Tu respondras: Meschant, point ne le croy,
> Car j'ay son cueur; & corps sans cueur, de foy
> Ne peult aymer; la raison y est bonne
>   S'il est ainsi.[35]

There is certainly nothing adventurous in the subject chosen here or in the form adopted for its expression; one notes in particular the presence of a typically French medieval figure in the guise of *Faulx rapport*, a figure which, incidentally, has no equivalent in the Italian original. C. S. Lewis makes the very necessary point with regard to the poetry of Sir Thomas Wyatt, the first of the English sixteenth-century Petrarchists:

> to translate Petrarch was not necessarily to introduce a new note into English poetry; it depended on the poems you chose and on the quality of your rendering. Thus Wyatt's 'Myne olde dere enmy my froward maister' is in fact a version of Petrarch's canzone *Quel antico mio dolce*; but the canzone . . . is so medieval, and Wyatt's version . . . is so like the rhyme royal of Hawes or Skelton, that if the original had been lost and Wyatt were not known to be the author, no one would dream of classifying the poem as anything but late medieval.[36]

In the case of the poem by Jean Marot, one notes that the theme of the lover leaving his heart with his lady as he goes away is a common one in the French poetic tradition; indeed, the expression of that theme in ll. 3–4, though quite clearly a translation of Serafino's 'el cor ti resta In cambio di mia fé', is exactly paralleled in a rondeau by Charles d'Orléans, which illustrates just how difficult it is to dissociate 'foreign' from 'native' elements in the poetry of the early sixteenth century. Charles d'Orléans's lines are addressed to Charles de Nevers on the occasion of the latter's departure from Blois:

> Pour paier vostre belle chiere,
> Laissez en gaige vostre cueur,
> Nous le garderons en doulceur
> Tant que vous retournez arriere.[37]

This while it is quite reasonable to suggest that French poets writing in the early sixteenth century may have been acquainted in one way or another with Italian love poetry, it is another thing to maintain that such acquaintance is of great importance in terms of French literary history. To take two examples from a *Chant-Royal* by Marot: the poet may well be alluding consciously to Petrarch in the opening lines:

> Prenant repos dessoubz ung vert Laurier
> Apres travail de noble Poesie . . .
>
> [*Œuvres Diverses*, No. 88]

But one assumes that even those who knew nothing at all of Petrarch's work might well have heard of his Laura/lauro puns. Similarly one can say that the refrain of this *Chant-Royal*

—'Desbender l'Arc ne guerist point la Playe'— undoubtedly
derives from Petrarch's 'piaga per allentar d'arco non sana', but
this is just the sort of line which might have existed
autonomously and proverbially. A knowledge of it does not
necessarily imply any further knowledge of Petrarch's work in
general. The line reappears in the 1534 edition of the
Hecatomphile and as l. 476 of Scève's *Saulsaye* in the form: 'L'arc
desbendé ne guerit pas la playe.'

Broadly speaking, therefore, I think one should resist the
application of the term Petrarchist to the poetry of Marot. Put
another way, the traditional view of Marot remains
substantially the correct one. L. Forster most recently
summarises it thus:

> Both Chaucer and Marot are poets firmly rooted in a native
> tradition. Both of them came into contact with Petrarchan
> influences, and made use of them to a minor extent. Neither of
> them can really be called a petrarchist. Moreover, they were not
> trying to forge a new poetic language; they had one already, which
> they and their public found entirely satisfactory.[38]

H. Weber makes a similar point with reference to Marot's
epigrams: 'Dans l'ensemble les épigrammes amoureuses de
Marot restent plus près de la tradition courtoise que du
pétrarquisme italien.'[39] There remains, of course, the possibility
that Petrarchism may have become acclimatised in France at a
very early stage. E. Parturier suggested as long ago as 1916 that
'le *Jardin de Plaisance* . . . renferme des pièces où l'on sent déjà
l'influence de Serafino'.[40] G. Tracconaglia, writing at about the
same time, put forward the view that 'notre influence artistique
[meaning Italian influence] se fait déjà timidement sentir dans les
vers de Christine de Pisan, de Charles d'Orléans'.[41] While M.
White thinks it probable that 'the stylized imagery and
intellectual conceits of early medieval French love poetry
entered French poetry anew from Italy at the very beginning of
the sixteenth century, elaborated and refined by Petrarch and
his Italian imitators'.[42] This is a possible line of enquiry, but I do
not think it can be a very fruitful one. In a poem like the Picart
rondeau quoted earlier one *may* be witnessing the result of a
Petrarchan stimulus acting on a traditional base, and this may
account for the differences between the Picart text and the
fifteenth-century examples quoted in connection with it.

Certainly it is logical that Petrarchism should first have exerted an influence in areas where the French and Italian traditions were already close together in terms of themes and devices. But at the same time, precisely because of this, I think it unlikely that one could ever distinguish effectively between the two. C. S. Lewis's comments on the misuse of the term *Renaissance* are instructive in the present context. He writes:

> as every attempt to define this mysterious character or quality turns out to cover all sorts of things that were there before the chosen period, a curious procedure is adopted. Instead of admitting that our definition has broken down, we adopt the desperate expedient of saying that 'the Renaissance' must have begun earlier than we thought. Thus Chaucer, Dante, and presently St Francis of Assisi, became 'Renaissance' men.[43]

Similar problems arise, it seems to me, in any attempt to push back the chronological limits of Petrarchism in France. Wherever one looks in the development of either late fifteenth-century or early sixteenth-century poetry there appears to be similar themes and devices in both French and Italian. I see no evidence at any point which would obviously indicate the presence of a new source of inspiration. When critics talk of 'Petrarchism' one should always enquire whether this is what they really mean and whether they have taken account of the great continuity which we have observed in the native French tradition. Of course the strength of the courtly movement in France had long been on the decline by the time the *Jardin* was published, but doubtless this is far more apparent in retrospect than it was to a contemporary audience. The Machaut ballade from which I quoted on page 21 may seem lifeless to us now, but it is typical of the sort of poetry which found favour in France over a very long period, and there seems no reason to suppose that it was less popular in 1500 than it had been a century earlier. So long as French love poetry was dominated by the debris of the courtly movement it could never progress; the disadvantages of the system are obvious to a modern reader, yet they were an integral part of the way that system functioned. The tendency towards abstraction, the love of cataloguing sentiments and of describing them in never-ending formulaic patterns—all this dates from at least as early as the thirteenth century, as some of the more uninspired passages in

the *Roman de la Rose* bear witness. Chartier's oxymoronic
description of the effects of love which I quoted in connection
with the theme of the icy fire, is indistinguishable from its
counterpart in the *Roman de la Rose*:

> Amour ce est pais haïneuse,
> Amour c'est haïne amoureuse;
> C'est leiautez la desleiaus,
> C'est la desleiautez leiaus;
> C'est peeur toute asseüree,
> Esperance desesperee . . .
>
> [ll. 4293 ff.]

And so it goes on, interminably. With 'Esperance desesperee'
we can move effortlessly over the two hundred and fifty years
or so which separates the *Roman de la Rose* from Marot's 'En
esperant, espoir me desespere', and at no point do we need to
invoke the ghosts of Petrarch or Petrarchism. It is all quite
solidly French and mediocre. Indeed, some may wish to argue
that the emotional range of which the courtly lyric is capable
found its fullest expression only in Occitaniah and Italian, and
that, though there were poets in France with a fine lyric sense,
from Conon de Béthune (*c.* 1150–1219) to Charles d'Orléans,
the   French   genius—and   the   English   too,   for   that
matter—revealed itself most naturally in the long narrative
poems, rather than in the short lyric forms that a poet such as
Bernard de Ventadour handled with such fluency. The
romances of Chrétien de Troyes, Chaucer's *Troilus and Criseyde*,
these are works which are profoundly affected by the courtly
tradition, but the courtly elements are only a contributing
factor, not the whole world of the poetry.

Whatever we may think of the French courtly tradition, we
must recognise that its influence survives well into the sixteenth
century and that its presence renders the task of any tracer of
literary influences a very delicate one. The difficulties are
further emphasised, moreover, when one considers the general
importance of oral sources. V.-L. Saulnier is one of the few
critics to draw attention to this. He writes:

> Il y a lieu de croire que les détails même de thèmes, images et
> figures, qui, chez tel poète, semblent provenir directement d'une
> source, ne venaient pas toujours d'une lecture: sauf le cas de

concordances répétées ou particulièrement frappantes. Une foule de thèmes, idées, métaphores, étaient dans le domaine commun.[44]

It might be possible, after a very detailed consideration of the available material, to imply that Petrarchism had the effect of consolidating and developing, in a very general and diffuse way, certain important themes and images in early sixteenth-century French poetry, but to try to distinguish in particular cases between what was native, what was borrowed, and what a combination of the two, seems a fruitless task. In the circumstances I think there is no reason to adopt the revised chronology of Petrarchan influence in France which C. A. Mayer has proposed and I think that any future attempts in this direction can succeed only if they take account of the problems raised by the existence of so many themes and devices that seem so ubiquitously shared.

2   The *Délie* of Maurice Scève

Moving forward chronologically, Scève is the most important French poet after Marot. Indeed it is sometimes held that Scève is the transitional key to the world which separates traditional French love poetry from the love lyrics of the Pléiade. Such a judgement seems to me if not indefensible then at least unhelpful, for the poetry of Scève at its best has little in common either with what preceded it or with what followed. At its worst it shares far more with the traditions of earlier poetry than with the lyrical excesses of the Pléiade and in general I think it scarcely points the way forward in any significant way, except possibly in the field of imagery, where Scève has been frequently, if again somewhat fruitlessly, compared with the nineteenth-century symbolists. The most thorough and reliable critic of Scève, V.-L. Saulnier, has called the poet the 'prince des rhétoriqueurs',[1] and this kind of attitude is representative of a particular strand of literary criticism, that which sees in the poetry of Scève, and especially in his dizain sequence *Délie*, certain qualities, though not generally of the first rank. I. D. McFarlane, in his edition of the *Délie*, shows himself to be a follower of this point of view, for he writes (p. 92): 'If . . . the attribute of greatness is to be granted only to those who have achieved range as well as perfection, Scève must rank among the finer of the *poetae minores*.' And in general I think this is a fair estimate of Scève's achievements. But over the last sixty years or so, attitudes towards the poet have swung wildly, from the almost totally hostile to the near idolatrous. Thus Eugène Parturier, who produced the first critical edition of the *Délie* in 1916, wrote in the following dismissive terms (p. xiii): 'La *Délie* est le plus obscur de tous les recueils pétrarquistes. On chercherait en vain, même en Italie, une poésie plus énigmatique, sauf peut-être quelques pièces particulièrement artificielles de Dante et de Pétrarque', while Georges Poulet, writing in 1967, expressed the modern position at its most extreme: 'C'est très délibérément que fut conçu ce livre [*Délie*] sous l'aspect d'un chapelet de petits poèmes tirant chacun la même réussite verbale d'un même conflit mental.'[2]

39

It is impossible to generalise in this way about a long sequence like the *Délie*, and Poulet's remarks in particular seem to me hopelessly undiscriminating. Some poems in the *Délie* are successful, others are not. Similarly it is important to place Parturier's comments on the obscurity of the collection in the proper perspective, or else they threaten to deter the boldest reader. There is indeed plenty of obscurity in the *Délie*, and plenty of artificiality too, but that is not the end of the matter. Formally the collection contains 449 poems, all in the form of dizains, that is to say poems ten lines in length. A preliminary huitain, entitled 'A Sa Délie', precedes the first dizain and it is accompanied by the motto 'Souffrir Non Souffrir', which is in reality an encapsulation of the old theme of the lover cherishing his suffering. All the lines in the *Délie* are decasyllabic rhyming ABABBCCDCD for the most part, though fifteen dizains have a different scheme. In this formal sense the collection belongs entirely to the conventions of its time. It first appeared in 1544 and a second edition followed twenty years later, by which time it must have seemed very much out of step with prevailing fashions. The title of the work has received some comment over the years. La Croix du Maine, writing in the late sixteenth century, was responsible for the anagrammatic interpretation of *Délie* as the Platonic *Idea* (= *L'Idée*), and this interpretation found favour until quite recently. Indeed it is still current in connection with Samuel Daniel's English sonnet sequence *Delia* (= *Ideal*), a collection first published in 1592 and the title of which probably owes something to the title of Scève's collection.[3] It is, however, unfashionable now to support any kind of anagrammatic interpretations in connection with Scève's dizains, on the grounds that the collection does not owe very much to the Platonic tradition, and that to insist on such a relationship would be to convey a limited impression of the work as a whole. I. D. McFarlane and D. G. Coleman have both drawn attention to the very wide-ranging associations of a name like *Délie*, while E. Giudici shows that it derives from a long poetic tradition with its roots in the classical past.[4] Poets such as Propertius, Tibullus, Ovid, and Virgil, and on the modern side, Chariteo (*c.* 1450–1514), Flaminio (1498–1550), and Tebaldeo (1463–1537), may all be cited in connection with Scève's choice of title. I am sure it is right not to insist on a narrow Platonic view of the *Délie*, but at the same time I do not think a sixteenth-century poet would have rejected an anagrammatic interpretation of his work. There was a widespread delight in such matters. I suppose we now find puns based on proper nouns rather naive, but the Greeks loved them: witness the 'pause of Pausanias' in Plato's *Symposium*; and in France we see the same kind of interest in Alain Chartier, 'the carter', and Molinet with his 'little mill', while on a rather different level we find the following conundrum explicitly attributed to Maurice Scève himself by É. Tabourot des Accords (1549–90), the 'Rabelais de la Bourgogne':

1 c 9 7 1 p a 10

This, being rendered into French, reads 'un con neuf, c'est un Paradis'.[5] I think, therefore, that all the possibilities of the name *Délie* would have been present in the mind of the poet. It is quite remarkable how poets tend to love women with poetically useful names. Of course, Petrarch may well have loved his Laura, and Scève may even have loved a woman whose family name was d'Heilly,[6] but they both took every advantage of the possibilities of these names, whatever the strict biographical situation may have been.

The dizain usually chosen to convey the range of associations offered by the name *Délie* is number 22:

Comme Hecaté tu me feras errer
Et vif, & mort cent ans parmy les Umbres:
Comme Diane au Ciel me resserrer,
D'ou descendis en ces mortelz encombres:
Comme regnante aux infernalles umbres
Amoindriras, ou accroistras mes peines.
　Mais comme Lune infuse dans mes veines
Celle tu fus, es, & seras DELIE,
Qu'Amour à joinct a mes pensées vaines
Si fort, que Mort jamais ne l'en deslie.[7]

Scève thus proclaims his everlasting love for Délie and there can be no commoner theme in love poetry than this. But if the theme is of great antiquity, I do not know any poet before Scève, in either France or Italy, who expresses his feelings in quite this way. Délie is identified here with Luna, Diana, and Hecate. She is the Moon-goddess; the goddess of hunting, the Greek Artemis, daughter of Zeus and sister of Apollo; she is Proserpine, the Greek Persephoné, wife of Pluto and queen of the underworld. The three goddesses are closely identified from classical times, but Scève makes the legends his own and personalises the whole mythological substructure. The living death which the lover traditionally endures is admirably conveyed in the image of the first two lines. The poet sees himself destined to wander through the lower world among the shades of the dead; but he is also the lover who has to accept the miseries of this world ('mortelz encombres'), and at the same time he can be drawn upwards by the elevating powers of the goddess. And, in the image of the waxing and waning moon, his sorrows depend on the varying attitudes towards him of the woman he loves. It is worth noting that there is no absolute correspondence between the three aspects of the goddess and the condition of the poet. Hecate and the underworld go together, of course, but in the succeeding four lines there is a deliberate fusion of three worlds, earth, heaven and hell; and Diana, Hecate, and Luna perform interchangeable functions, so that there is a waxing and waning even in hell. The concluding lines of the poem are among the most famous in the *Délie*. The moon as goddess flows through the poet's veins and he is tied to Délie for ever. The image is, I think, unique. Parturier points out that Chariteo also identified his beloved with Luna, but that is not the point. The Italian poet simply says that his lady holds in her hands both life and death, that he has shed all his tears in vain, and that his beloved is thus rightly called the moon goddess ('E con justa cagion chiamata Luna . . . '). The identification in the Scève poem is total and has more power than that of simple mythological allusion.

At the same time I think one can see in dizain 22 an illustration of something common to the majority of the poems in the *Délie*, that is a tendency towards unevenness, both of syntax and of tone. Lines 3–6 show an attempt to modify the syntactic pattern which appears to be establishing itself very simply from the beginning. 'Comme Diane . . . ' exactly parallels 'Comme Hecaté . . . ' and I think Ronsard would have continued in the same fashion at l. 5, for there is a marked formal neatness about Ronsard's sonnets, a point to which F. Desonay calls attention and to which I shall return in the final section of this book.[8] Scève, however, is looking for variation at l. 5, and though I think he achieves an interesting effect in this example the desire for variety is by no means always beneficial

to the musical quality of the verse in the *Délie*. Then one notes
the juxtaposition of the rhetorical commonplace in l. 8 'Celle tu
fus, es, & seras DELIE' beside the preceding line which is one of
the finest of the whole collection. Again, on balance, the effect
works in context, but it does draw attention to the fact that
Scève has been judged a poet of fine lines, rather than of fine
poems. H. Weber writes: 'La poésie n'est presque jamais chez
lui d'une seule coulée, d'un jaillissement continu; s'il est capable
d'animer le dizain d'un mouvement sobre et vigoureux, les
beaux vers surgissent comme des blocs étincelants au milieu d'un
ensemble rugueux.'⁹ One notes too considerable variation in the
attitudes of sixteenth-century readers of Scève, and while this
may not of course derive from the highest of motives, it may
reflect similar reactions to those of Weber. Often quoted in this
context is the following poem by Charles Fontaine, which
appeared in 1546; he addresses the author of the *Délie* in these
terms:

> Tes vers sont beaux & bien luysants,
> Graves & pleins de majesté,
> Mais pour leur haulteur moins plaisants:
> Car certes la difficulté
> Le grand plaisir en a osté.
> Brief ilz ne quierent un lecteur,
> Mais la commune autorité
> Dit qu'ilz requierent un docteur.¹⁰

The attitude of the Pléiade towards Scève was a very ambiguous
one, and there is a useful summary of the details in A.
Boulanger's edition of the *Art Poëtique* of Jacques Peletier du
Mans.¹¹ The positive side of the Pléiade reaction can be seen in
the one hundred and fifth sonnet of the *Olive*, du Bellay's first
collection of poetry, which appeared four years after the
publication of the *Délie*. Du Bellay addresses Scève as follows:

> Si de ton bruit ma Lire enamourée
> Ta gloire encor' ne va point racontant,
> J'aime, j'admire & adore pourtant
> Le hault voler de ta plume dorée.

In the opening of this sonnet Scève is referred to as 'Esprit
divin', while in the following sonnet Ronsard is invoked simply
as 'noble esprit', though I would not wish to make much of that.

One of the finest poems in the *Délie* to my mind is dizain 175,

and it provides a rare instance where a comparison between
Scève and the nineteenth-century symbolists has something
interesting to offer. The opening lines of the poem read as
follows:

> Voy le jour cler ruyner en tenebres,
> Ou son bienfaict sa clarté perpetue:
> Joyeux effectz finissent en funebres,
> Soit que plaisir contre ennuy s'esvertue.

The difficult and seemingly abstract presentation here in fact
conceals a definite physical reality, and this is in itself of
considerable significance. For, as I shall show later, Scève very
often seems more concerned to analyse his inner conflicts in the
traditional abstract manner, rather than to seek convincing
expression for those conflicts by relating them to something
outside himself. The best critics to follow for the elucidation of
the opening lines of dizain 175 are P. Boutang and H. Weber,
not because they necessarily provide the 'correct' reading, but
because they offer an interpretation which is poetically
convincing and which does not exclude the possible addition of
further elements.[12] The poet watches the aftermath of the sun's
disappearance and the lingering patterns of light ('Joyeux
effectz') which are also doomed to disappear in their turn, just as
a happy day of festivities is bound to pass eventually, leaving a
feeling of emptiness and melancholy behind, however much one
may try to prolong the pleasure of the moment. Even the
shadow of that which is bright cannot last. The language is
consciously abstract, *bienfaict*, *effectz*, *plaisir*, *ennuy*, but a positive
image does emerge from this abstraction, an image which is not
precisely definable, but capable of variation according to the
temperament of the individual reader. The opening line gains
much of its evocative power from the verb *ruyner* and I imagine
the use of the verb would have been as striking to a
contemporary reader as it is to a modern one, for there seem to
be no other examples of a comparable intransitive use in Scève's
time. *Ruyner* in the sense of 'to fall' is not illustrated in Huguet's
dictionary of sixteenth-century French until *c.* 1584, and though
Godefroy's Old French dictionary lists a number of intransitive
uses of the verb, they are quite unrelated to Scève's technique
here.[13] The fusion of abstract and concrete which we find at the

beginning of dizain 175 is pursued throughout the poem with an insistence that is rare in the *Délie*; ll. 5–8 read as follows:

> Toute haultesse est soubdain abatue,
> De noz deduitz tant foible est le donneur.
> Et se crestantz les arbres, leur honneur,
> Legere gloire, en fin en terre tumbe . . .

This could well serve as an illustration of Mallarmé's dictum 'peindre non la chose, mais l'effet qu'elle produit'. As McFarlane suggests in his notes on this poem, *se crestantz* contains more than the idea of 's'élever, grandir', which is how Parturier glosses the term in his edition of the *Délie*: the idea of 'crest, foliage' is there too. 'Leur honneur' would thus apply to the leaves of the tree which are doomed, however beautiful ('legere gloire'), to fall. The leaves are not mentioned as physical objects, but only in terms of the sensation they produce in the observer. This enhances the appeal of the concluding lines:

> Ou ton hault bien aura seul ce bon heur
> De verdoyer sur ta fameuse tombe.[14]

The moral attribute of Délie's virtue ('ton hault bien') remains an abstraction directly fused with a physical impression, there being no need for the establishment of any formal link. McFarlane suggests that the whole dizain may be read as an invocation to Petrarch's Laura, but I see no reason why the 'fameuse tombe' should not be that of Délie. It is true that Scève played a part in the events surrounding the supposed discovery of Laura's tomb in Avignon, but it seems to me that dizain 175 looks to the future and not the past in its final two lines, and if the invocation is indeed to Laura it is an extremely subtle one. One might compare the references to Petrarch himself in dizains 417 or 388, where Scève leaves us in no doubt of the identity of his Tuscan hero:

> Donc ce Thuscan pour vaine utilité
> Trouve le goust de son Laurier amer:
> Car de jeunesse il aprint a l'aymer.

[dizain 388]

The *Délie* has a certain general interest for the literary historian because it is the first sequence in French, dedicated to a single woman in the manner that was to prove extraordinarily popular during the sixteenth century. The desire to produce such a sequence almost certainly derives from Italian influence. Though Petrarch's *Canzoniere* is not formally dedicated to Laura (its original title is simply *Rerum vulgarium fragmenta*, which gave way early on to *Canzoniere*, or 'song book'), the possibilities which Petrarch revealed of immortalising both oneself and one's beloved though the creation of a series of poems were bound to act as a spur to any poet who took the craft of the love lyric at all seriously. Du Bellay, in the opening sonnet of the *Olive*, alludes specifically to the analogy between his olive and Petrarch's laurel,[15] looking forward to the day when, as the result of his poetic endeavours, the two can be seen as equally glorious. As in ancient times the laurel and the olive were both a symbol of glory to those who received them, so Laura and Olive will one day stand side by side. We have seen that Scève's Délie derives her name from the mythological rather than the botanical, but there is little doubt that, whatever Scève's own direct knowledge of Petrarch's work may have been, the impulse to publish a sequence must have stemmed from the example of the *Canzoniere*.

Of course, the fact that the *Délie* is a sequence in no way proves that Scève's original intention in writing poetry was to compose such a sequence. He may well have decided to group a number of isolated poems together under the name of his beloved at a fairly late stage, and in fact I think this is probably what happened. However many efforts are expended to deomonstrate the contrary, there is no formal unity in the *Délie*, as there is for example in the *Olive*. Both the first and last sonnets of du Bellay's collection end with the same reference to the laurèl/Laura ambiguity, and the poems in between are closely related to the description of the love experience. I think Scève's *Délie*, like Petrarch's *Canzoniere*, was a long time in the making; both collections contain poems on a variety of non-amatory subjects and while some of these are obviously designed to provide a change of tone, some of those in Scève's collection at least are probably survivals from a very early period. H. Jacoubet writes: 'il y a des dixains de Scève datés par des allusions qui nous font remonter à 1526–1527. Mais une remarque importante: dans aucun de ces dixains il n'est question de Délie', to which Giudici adds the comment: 'Il che fa pensare che Scève abbia incorporato nella *Délie dizains* isolati e scritti precedentemente, quando ancora non aveva cominciato lo sostanziale stesura del poema.'[16] There would be nothing strange in that. Everyone knows that Petrarch first saw Laura on Good Friday in 1327, but he was certainly writing lyric verse in the vernacular before that date. In his notes to dizains 19–21 of the *Délie* McFarlane suggests similarly that these few poems at least may well be much older than the others in the collection, for the events which they describe—the defection of the Connétable de Bourbon to the cause of Francis I's enemies—started over twenty years before the publication of the *Délie* in 1544. In general, however, McFarlane would place the bulk of the poems in the *Délie* at some point in the 1530s, probably from about 1537 onwards.

The dizains which do not deal with amatory subjects exclusively are not very large in number, certainly less than 10 per cent of the total, and none of them, I think, show Scève at his best. Dizain 28 is obscure, but is apparently concerned with a visit to Marseille by the pope, Clement VII, in 1533; dizains 53–5, 252–3, and 323 all contain a reference to Francis I; No. 85 deals with the execution of one of Henry VIII's wives, almost certainly Catherine Howard, though Marcel Françon suggests Ann Boleyn;[17] dizains 115, 298, 389, and 437 all refer to Charles-Quint; No. 147 to the death of Sir Thomas More; Nos. 254–5 centre on Francis I's sister, Marguerite de Navarre; No. 305 refers to the death of Erasmus and Lefèvre d'Etaples in 1536:

> Aussi cest An par Mort, qui tout abrege,
> France perdit ce, qu'à perdu Hollande.

Dizain 318 refers to the truce of Nice in 1538 between France, Italy, and Spain; No. 416 contains an obscure allusion to king James V of Scotland; No. 432 refers to the Archduke Ferdinand; while the penultimate dizain in the collection returns to the figure of Charles-Quint. This latter poem is the best of the so-called historical dizains, for, unlike a poem such as dizain 21, the historical allusion is fully integrated into the love experience that is the major interest of the *Délie*.[18] Scève draws a comparison between the failure of Charles-Quint's hopes at the seige of Landrecy (1543)—at which, interestingly enough, the English poet Henry Howard, Earl of Surrey, was present, four years before he was executed—and the bitterness which he feels about the love he has been describing:

Vouloir tousjours, ou le povoir est moindre,
Que la fortune, & tousjours persister
Sans au debvoir de la raison se joindre,
Contre lequel on ne peult resister,
Seroit ce pas au danger assister,
Et fabriquer sa declination?
Seroit ce pas, sans expectation
D'aulcun acquest, mettre honneur a mercy,
Ou bien jouer sa reputation
Pour beaucoup moins, qu'a Charles Landrecy?[19]

R. Mulhauser offers the following extraordinary misreading of the poem: 'though it seems superficially negative and skeptical, [it] is in reality a beautiful, modest victory poem through its allusion to Francis's wise patience at Landrécies which brought Francis-Scève, the spiritual lover, final victory over Charles Quint-Scève, the carnal lover.'[20] Such an interpretation derives from a desire to show an evolution over the *Délie* as a whole, moving from a supposedly youthful state of aberration and infatuation in the early poems of the sequence to a state of spiritual illumination on the part of the poet at the end. But there seems to be no evidence to support such an evolutionary view. On the contrary, I think the placing of what is in effect a highly sceptical poem in the penultimate position of the sequence is a lesson in the fact that love is not, as a rule, given to mathematical progressions. Scève sees that to attempt to pursue his love in circumstances that are unfavourable is bound to lead to personal ruin. The old contrast between love and reason which is common to all ages, and to none more so than the medieval period, is reiterated by Scève and the conclusion he must come to is an obvious one. Reason alone is a trustworthy authority; and love appears, as it does in the second part of the *Roman de la Rose*, as a false master who inspires blind passions to send men to their destruction.

Scève's love is almost entirely a thing of this world and we have Petrarch's warnings on the subject from the very beginning of the *Canzoniere*:

e del mio vaneggiar vergogna è 'l frutto
e 'l pentersi, e 'l conoscer chiaramente
che quanto piace al mondo è breve sogno.[21]

Scève seems to have realised no more than this when almost at the end of his sequence and there is something moving in that, perhaps. Yet he is not really close to Petrarch in the penultimate dizain of the *Délie*. He is not rejecting earthly love in a general sense, simply questioning, in a realistic way, whether for him the effort is worthwhile. One senses that if he had received or could conceive of receiving some profit or advantage ('acquest') from his experiences in love, he would not mind exposing his honour and reputation, and this is the disillusionment of the worldly man, not of the spiritual. This whole affair has been important, perhaps, but far less so than he or the reader would have thought, of far less significance than the seige of Landrecy was for Charles-Quint, at all events. Some things in this world, at least, have a significance that can be measured objectively, even if love is not one of them—so doubtless it seemed to Scève, writing this penultimate dizain as he must have done, only a few months after the historical event which it describes.

The attempt to impose structural or thematic unities on a sequence is common enough on the part of critics and is usually doomed to failure for the most obvious reasons. The problems of organising a sequence are considerable and one should never lose sight of that fact in one's search for formal neatness and precision. L. Harvey, while recognising that even so short a sequence as the sonnet collection of Louise Labé fails to display any real narrative coherence, seeks to establish a kind of unity which he thinks derives from 'the longing for immutability in the realm of the transient'.[22] He adds: 'The individual sonnet, with its sharply defined architecture, provides a formal solidity that can represent admirably this desired immutability', and other critics have written in similar vein about the structure of the dizain. But such a line of enquiry is so general that it seems a mere desperate clutching at straws. I think that Donald Stone's book on *Ronsard's Sonnet Cycles*, although in many respects an excellent work, also suffers from a tendency to impose unities where none exist. Stone traces a line from what he considers to be the inferior poems in the *Amours* of 1552–3 to what he sees as the more balanced products of the *Sonets pour Helene*. He writes: 'for his final cycle, Ronsard was keenly sensitive to certain problems of structure and presentation which had long been ignored in favor of stylistic and thematic problems.'[23] Stone's evolutionary view of Ronsard's poetry inevitably forces him to draw general conclusions about the superiority or inferiority of

particular cycles that could never be supported on a detailed
level by the evidence of individual sonnets. Even when
considering the *Olive*, which, as I have suggested, does reveal a
fair degree of formal unity, one should be careful about pushing
one's desire for coherence too far. Thus G. Saba puts forward a
view concerning the differences between the first and second
editions of the *Olive* which once again could only be justified in
the most vague and general sense. Saba writes:

> Se la prima edizione dell' *Olive* . . . discopre una preoccupazione
> ancora estrinseca, la seconda mostra d' essere l'espressione d'una
> visione armonica, onde i sonetti, non piú disgiunti nell' insieme,
> sono le note indispensabili di un canto compiuto.[24]

In fact one is usually going to find considerable problems in
any attempt to treat a sequence as if it were some kind of early
novel. As C. S. Lewis points out: 'The first thing to grasp about
the sonnet sequence is that it is not a way of telling a story. It is a
form which exists for the sake of a prolonged lyrical medita-
tion.'[25] One of the consequences of this is that the reader does not
have to worry about finding a progression within a sequence,
nor is there necessarily any need to try to resolve the conflicts and
contradictions which any sequence will inevitably set before him.
As we have seen the penultimate dizain of the *Délie* is highly
sceptical and bitter in tone. The final poem, on the other hand,
is a much more positive affair, but I do not think one should
make too much of that. Scève ends his collection on a note of
peace, but this does not deny the validity of everything that
has gone before: any resolution of conflict or diminution of
bitterness is, one feels, only temporary, and that is one of the
most interesting things about a sequence. No one, I hope,
would have tried to read a collection like the *Délie* from
beginning to end. A sequence is the kind of work into which
you can dip at odd moments, to find some poem that matches
your mood at the time, to spark off some new train of thought,
or quite simply to find something that will amuse you. Fulfilling
the demands of the latter category is dizain 221:

> Sur le Printemps, que les Aloses montent,
> Ma Dame, & moy saultons dans le batteau,
> Ou les Pescheurs entre eulx leur prinse comptent,
> Et une en prent: qui sentant l'air nouveau,
> Tant se debat, qu'en fin se saulve en l'eau,

> Dont ma Maistresse & pleure, & se tourmente.
>   Cesse: luy dy je, il fault que je lamente
> L'heur du Poisson, que n'as sceu attraper,
> Car il est hors de prison vehemente,
> Ou de tes mains ne peuz onc eschapper.

Only the most dedicated lovers of Platonic explanations could take this delightful poem seriously. A.-M. Schmidt provides an interpretation which reads like a parody of the academic approach to poetry; he writes:

> Quoique rapportant un fait réel, l'intention symbolique de ce dizain n'en est pas moins évidente: en effet, le poisson est un emblème à la fois vénusiaque et christique, dont l'apparition signifie que Scève, échappant plus tard à l'amour de Pernette, bien que comblé de grâces par celui-là, accédera à la plénitude de la rédemption.[26]

However that may be, I trust a contemporary reader would have been amused by Scève's anecdote. The *Aloses*, according to the Larousse, are rather like sardines and they travel up river in the spring to spawn. This indication of the season in the opening line recalls a very long European tradition of spring love songs and doubtless a sixteenth-century reader would have expected some lyrical evocation to follow. But the mention of the fish turns out to be more relevant than one thought, for the whole poem centres on the differing fates of the poet, who is a prisoner of Délie, and the fish, which manages, however inelegantly, to escape her. Though there is no seriousness here one could easily imagine the theme transformed in a different context. But Scève merely wishes to indulge in a little self-mockery. He could never behave like the fish, for that would be far too unseemly. At the same time, he manages to disagree with his beloved, who is excessively chagrined at the course of events, and even to strike an unusually familiar note, precisely because there is a recognition on all sides that he is not serious. One must take any opportunities for such playfulness that present themselves, for they are rare in the *Délie*.

I have already mentioned that the final dizain in Scève's sequence ends on a positive note and it would be as well to clarify this. R. D. Cottrell sees in the conclusion of the *Délie* the 'ultimate resolution [of the poet's passion] in an ecstatic contemplation of the eternal', while I. D. McFarlane notes that 'the sequence ends with the sublimation of passion into spiritual certainty and tranquillity'.[27] Here is the poem:

> Flamme si saincte en son cler durera,
> Tousjours luysante en publicque apparence,
> Tant que ce Monde en soy demeurera,
> Et qu'on aura Amour en reverence.
>   Aussi je voy bien peu de différence
> Entre l'ardeur, qui noz cœurs poursuyvra,
> Et la vertu, qui vive nous suyvra
> Oultre le Ciel amplement long, & large.
>   Nostre Genevre ainsi doncques vivra
> Non offensé d'aulcun mortel Letharge.[28]

Scève indeed seems to end his sequence quite clearly on the theme of the immortality of a love which finds its ultimate resolution in heaven, but there is more to the poem than that. Of course final poems almost inevitably draw one towards transcendental solutions, and the image of the evergreen juniper-tree in the penultimate line—the exact counterpart of du Bellay's olive—is entirely satisfying in this respect. But what Scève is seeking is, I think, not so much transcendence or sublimation as a kind of reconciliation, a solution to the problems of sensual love that does not entail a complete victory for the spiritual viewpoint.[29] The key line in this connection is the fifth, for there Scève appears to give the impression of logical argument, while in fact he is arguing very much from a position of self-interest. The two main sections of the poem, of four lines each, are related to the final two lines by the word *ainsi* which gives a general overall impression of something uncontroversial and reasonably argued, but Scève is trying to show (in ll. 5–8) that there is, in reality, very little difference between *la vertu* and *l'ardeur*, and this is, of course, by no means self-evident or logically proven in the context of the poem. Scève could so easily have placed virtue and beauty on the same plane; or he could have contrived a respectful ending to parallel that which Petrarch gives to the *Canzoniere* and in which we find the standard vocabulary of love-longing, *mercede, guerra, belli occhi, lagrime, sospiri* and all the rest, turned towards the Virgin and away from earthly objects in a moving plea for forgiveness for his attachment to Laura. But instead Scève chooses to reconcile two forms of love that are apparently contradictory and to grant the same immortality both to the sensuous and the spiritual. There are plenty of examples of this kind of approach elsewhere in the *Délie*, but it is not the same as an ecstatic contemplation of the eternal. In a simple way, one might be tempted to see in the contrast between Petrarch's final poem and the ending of the *Délie* the distance which separates medieval from Renaissance man, but I think that what is more important is simply the difference in temperament between the two poets.

Petrarch's plea is intensely moving, full of fear at approaching death, and completely dominated by the realisation of the superiority of divine over human love. Chaucer's Troilus also attains this realisation, though it is far less moving in context. In his retreat into the eighth sphere, Troilus looks down on the world he has left, the source of all that is transitory and hence of all unhappiness:

> And down from thennes faste he gan avyse   [*gaze upon*
> This litel spot of erthe, that with the se   [*sea*
> Embraced is, and fully gan despise
> This wrecched world, and held al vanite
> To respect of the pleyn felicite   [*compared with*
> That is in hevene above . . .
>
> [bk. v, ll. 1814–19]

For the devout, or even averagely aware, medieval reader, there could be no question that ultimately the things of this world were not to be trusted and that it was sinful to hold on to them. The greater your capacity for love, the more you needed to ensure that it was properly directed, for in a man of refinement love for a woman could appear to approach the level of the divine, and thus the potential for sinful attachment was all the greater.

The reliance on transcendental solutions to the problems of earthly love lingers on for a long time. Thus Bernardino Daniello, in a sonnet which du Bellay translated ('Si nostre vie est moins qu'une journée . . .'), ends his poem with the following reference to heaven:

> Ivi è quel sommo ben ch'ogni huom desìa;
> Ivi 'l vero riposo; ivi la pace
> Ch' indarno tu quagiù cercando vai.[30]

And of course such an attitude can reappear at any time, given
the appropriate temperament. But arguably it was never a very
characteristic feature of French Renaissance love poetry. É.
Faguet, writing on Ronsard's debt to Petrarch, suggests that
what Ronsard took from the *Canzoniere* was a sense of 'les
délicatesses de l'amour pur, respectueux, élevé sans être sublime',
and he adds, 'C'est, je crois, le degré de Platonisme où les
Français, qui ne mêlent presque jamais aucun mysticisme à leurs
sentiments, peuvent atteindre.'[31] Certainly in the final dizain of
the *Délie* there is a stress on the immortality of love in heaven,
but this is not, I think, at the expense of the pleasures of this
world, and one may recall in this context the remark which A.
Glauser made with reference to dizain 408 of Scève's collection:
'Comme la volupté a été défendue au poète dans la vie . . . il la
souhaite dans la mort.'[32] It is also interesting to note how du
Bellay modifies the sonnet by Daniello that I have just quoted,
for it provides a further illustration of Faguet's point of view.
Again referring to heaven, du Bellay writes:

> La, est le bien que tout esprit desire,
> La, le repos ou tout le monde aspire,
> La, est l'amour, la le plaisir encore.
>
> [ll. 9–11]

Where Daniello looks for a totally spiritual enjoyment, du
Bellay attempts to fuse the terrestial and the spiritual so that he
can look forward to love and even to pleasure. Of course, these
two words do not necessarily imply any specific sensual
prospects in the world to come, but, as in the final dizain of the
Délie, they leave open the possibility that heaven will provide
the enjoyment of worldly things, at a superior and continuous
level, rather than suggesting that the superior level is simply the
love of God and not of woman. In this sense, one of the most
problematic issues raised by the courtly tradition finds some sort
of a solution, clearly a solution based on wish-fulfilment, but
something quite different from what one finds in Petrarch or
Dante or in Chaucer's repudiation of his Troilus and 'many a
leccherous lay'. In general I do not think that Scève is
particularly drawn to Christian or even markedly spiritual
resolutions in the *Délie*, and the collection is thus rather more
than 'a long poem in obscure and learned dizains on sublimated
love', as *The Oxford Companion to French Literature*, not
untypically, puts it.

Of course, spiritual interpretations can be hard to resist. Santayana says: 'In some form or other Platonic ideas occur in all poetry of passion when it is seasoned with reflection',[33] but only, I think, in that sense could the *Délie* be described as a Platonic sequence. Some of the finest lines in the collection are those in which the realisation of chances missed in this world is brought openly, and without any hope of transcendence, before the reader. Thus from dizain 310 we have the reflection:

> Je n'auray eu de ta verte jeunesse . . .
> Sinon rameaulx, & fueilles tresameres.

And this kind of directness is characteristic of a number of Scève's best-known poems. Witness the often-quoted lines from dizain 161:

> Seul avec moy, elle avec sa partie:
> Moy en ma peine, elle en sa molle couche.
> Couvert d'ennuy je me voultre en l'Ortie,
> Et elle nue entre ses bras se couche.

The possibility that not all that many of the poems in the *Délie* may accurately reflect the sub-title of the work, *Délie: Object de plus haulte vertu*, that, in other words, Scève is very often concerned with the practical problems of *sensuous* love, has only been considered in relatively recent times. I think it would be possible to show that much of the *Délie* relies on the ambiguous language of the courtly tradition, the principles of which I discussed in the opening section of this book, and the presence of this deliberate ambiguity has been responsible for the persistence of interpretations which unduly stress the spiritual nature of the work. To take a very simple example: in the opening huitain, Scève claims that he is not interested in the 'ardentz estincelles' of Venus or the arrows of Cupid, but only in '. . . les mortz, qu'en moy tu renovelles.' Because Scève rejects the figures most closely identified with sensual love, it is easy to assume that he is therefore interested in its opposite, that pure love which Parturier relates to the closing pages of Castiglione's *Cortegiano*. But the use of the noun *les mortz* is deliberately ambiguous; it can suggest anything from the purest to the most debased attitudes and had long been used in the European tradition to cover the complete range of emotions and

sensations. Troilus immediately thinks of death in connection
with his new-found love for Criseyde:

> Love, ayeins the which whoso defendeth   [*against*
> Hymselven most, hym alderlest avaylleth,   [*least of all*
> With disespeyr so sorwfulli me offendeth,   [*attacks*
> That streight unto the deth myn herte sailleth.
>
> [bk. i, ll. 603–6]

And later (bk. II, ll. 337 ff.), Pandarus asks Criseyde to save
Troilus from death, from which it is clear to all that he wishes
her to become Troilus's lover. At its most sensual the word *mort*
can mean nothing more (or less) than 'orgasm', the noun
sometimes being modified, as in the Italian 'piccola morte'.
While on the other hand the notion of love as a living death can
be treated with the utmost seriousness in the hands of certain
writers. Guido Cavalcanti (*c.* 1255–1300) is one of these, and in
his canzone beginning 'Donna me prega' he analyses the way in
which love can prove fatal to the man who is possessed by it.
Love is a force which invariably results in a turning away from
reason and a complete loss of control and because, for
Cavalcanti, reason is the key to life, the highest good, anyone
who abandons its tenets will inevitably die within himself:

> Di sua potenza segue spesso morte,
> se forte — la vertù fosse impedita,
> la quale aita — la contraria via:
> non perché oppost' a naturale sia:
>   ma quanto che da buon perfetto tort' è
> per sorte, — non pò dire om ch'aggia vita,
> ché stabilita — non ha segnoria.[34]

Thus behind Scève's use of the simple noun *mortz* there lies an
extremely long tradition and it is important to bear this in mind
before attempting to define the specific nature of the love he is
celebrating.

If one looks again at the final dizain of the *Délie* one can see in
Scève's use of the adjective *saincte* ('Flamme si saincte') another
example of a deliberately ambiguous approach to vocabulary.
The adjective seems to indicate a specific attitude towards love
and yet if one examines other occurrences of the word in the
Délie it becomes clear that it has in reality no fixed connotation,

no necessary connection with pure Christian or Platonic love. An interesting example occurs in dizain 376. One finds there an account of the poet's dependence on his beloved: 'Tu es le Corps, Dame, & je suis ton umbre', and this sense of a close harmony is maintained until the last two lines, when Scève suddenly reveals an exception:

Fors que je sens trop inhumainement
Noz sainctz vouloirs estre ensemble discords.

Clearly there is something contrived in this expression of discord in harmony, an attempt to produce a series of antitheses which can contain the maximum power of ambiguous suggestion. The poet reveals that he and Délie really desire different things, but he applies the adjective *sainctz* to both sides, as though to justify both points of view. Délie's *vouloir* may be described in these lofty terms inasmuch as she may favour a chaste relationship with the poet; the poet, on the other hand, may use the same adjective to describe his own feelings because he does not accept that physical love is inevitably sinful, quite the contrary. I have already commented on the ambiguous use of the noun *vouloir* in my discussion of the troubadour Bernard de Ventadour and Scève is working on exactly the same level: the *will* of the lady and the *desire* of the poet may indeed be 'ensemble discords'. Saulnier, though he believes in the eventual Platonic resolution of Scève's sequence, has drawn attention to the ambiguous use of a number of common words in the *Délie*. He notes the ambiguity in such expressions as '*chastes* prieres' or 'l'ardent désir du *haut* bien désiré', and he comments: 'Ne soyons pas dupes. Ce grand bien que souhaite le poète recouvre, dans les termes, une équivoque commode . . . l'on surprend . . . sous bien des formules d'allure polie, tout autre chose qu'un attachement de vertu . . . Saint, chaste, loyal: tout cela est plus vite dit que pensé.'[35] It is important to remember that this kind of deliberate ambiguity is not something confined to Scève's poetry; it draws its principles from the very nature of the kind of poetry he is writing. Thus Weber, commenting on the frequent use of the expression 'haut bien' and similar constructions with the adjective *haut*, misses a part of the essential context when he says: 'Cette obsession de l'adjectif "haut" exprime . . . fort bien l'élévation de la pensée qui est pour Scève la démarche essentielle de l'amour.'[36]

Expressions involving an ambiguous use of the word *haut* are
common long before the *Délie* and Scève's own practice is in no
way abnormal. One may compare the following lines from a
poem published in Langlois's *Documents inédits sur l'histoire de
France*:

> Pour avoir paix et parfaitte plaisance,
> Doit vrais amans en son cuer affermer
> Que dame tient et a en gouvernance
> Touz les haulz dons qu'Amours a a donner.

> [p. 24]

The phrase 'haulz dons', like the expression 'haulz biens', which
occurs later in the poem, is used exactly in the way Scève would
use it, and the most casual glance at a collection of fifteenth-
century poems will show that phrases such as 'hault plaisir',
'haultain plaisir', 'hault guerredon', 'biens haultains', and so on,
are extemely popular and belong to a flourishing tradition. If a
writer wished to conceal a sensual intent, there was no better
way than to surround his longings with decorous phrases, as in
the following lines from the *Jardin*:

> Puis qu'ainsi est que ne puis parvenir
> Aux haultains biens de mon doulx souvenir
> Finer me fault mes jours prouchainement . . .

> [fo. xcv]

Because we are so completely divorced from the society which
delighted in this kind of poetic ambiguity we doubtless miss
many ironic or witty allusions in trying to reconstitute the
poetic milieu. One has to be constantly awake to the
possibilities which the language of the courtly tradition
provides. Thus Saulnier says of the poetry of Pernette du
Guillet: 'du plaisir sensuel, elle ne parle pas une fois';[37] but the
most recent editor of her work quite rightly points to lines such
as the following which are clearly of sensuous intent:

> O que le faict doit estre grandement
> Remply de bien, quand pour la grand envie
> On veult mourir, s'on ne l'a promptement:
> Mais ce mourir engendre une autre vie.[38]

Quite recognisably the world of 'la piccola morte', in fact.

And so in the *Délie* one finds numerous examples of this ambiguous use of abstract language. In a poem such as dizain 90 one seems safe in assuming a spiritual intent:

Par ce hault bien, qui des Cieulx plut sur toy,
Tu m'excitas du sommeil de paresse

while in dizain 82 a sensual one:

L'ardent desir du hault bien desiré,
Qui aspiroit a celle fin heureuse

but in the nature of things one can never really be sure whether one or other implication is dominant. Expressions such as 'hault bien', 'hault vouloir' (dizains 240, 421), 'haulte victoyre' (249), 'hault penser' (118, 414), 'hault desir' (274), 'haulte poursuyte' (296), and so on, often seem merely confusing to a modern reader, whereas I think they were an immediate source of delight to those in the know. 'Je veulx perir en si haulte poursuyte', Scève writes at the end of dizain 296, and we are in the middle of a highly sophisticated erotic world. Saulnier notes the phrase 'le bien du bien'—a further refinement!—in the poetry of Pernette du Guillet, and equates it with 'le souverain bien de Platon', while H. Staub notes that the very same phrase in dizain 133 of the *Délie* has profoundly sensual implications:

Lors je sentis distiler en mon ame
Le bien du bien, qui tout aultre surmonte.[39]

Certainly a modern reader can make little sense out of such lines as the following from dizain 406, though they are obviously concerned with the relationship between physical and spiritual love:

Haultain vouloir en si basse pensée,
Haulte pensée en un si bas vouloir . . .

And I think the modern reader can never really share in the sense of game and high seriousness which underlies the widely recurring alternations of *vie* and *mort* in the *Délie*, as in such phrases as 'Mort de ma mort, & vie de ma vie' in dizain 167. But we should at least be prepared to follow the sophistication of this kind of poetry as far as we can, even if we do tend to lose our way in the terminology. We can at least be alive, for example, to the very subtle wit of the following lines, something which has not, to my knowledge, ever been commented upon before:

> Si ne te puis pour estrenes donner
> Chose, qui soit selon toy belle, & bonne,
> Et que par faict on ne peult guerdonner
> Un bon vouloir, comme raison l'ordonne,
>   Au moins ce don je le presente, & donne,
> Sans aultre espoir d'en estre guerdonné:
> Qui, trop heureux ainsi abandonné,
> Est, quant a toy, de bien petite estime:
>   Mais, quant a moy, qui tout le t'ay donné,
> C'est le seul bien, apres toy, que j'estime.

[dizain 205]

The poet muses over a new-year's gift for his beloved, and he says: 'If I cannot give you something which is, like you, beautiful and good, and if indeed it is not possible to reward an honest desire, even though reason demands that one should, at least I can present you with this gift . . .'. The pronoun *on* is here (l. 3) deliberately ambiguous, but we are clearly in the world of courtly *vouloir* and *guerdons*, with all the potential connotations of sexuality which underlie these terms. The poet insists, however, that the mere giving of the gift, which is in fact the poem we are reading, is all the reward he seeks; and the poem itself is only too happy to be abandoned by its creator and delivered into the hands of the beloved, even though she is not terribly impressed with its merits. But then, the poet says, in a final subtle comment, I am the one who has given you the poem and I have given it to you totally, so for me it is the only good which I value, after you yourself. He values his poem because it is his and because it now belongs to his beloved. The ambiguities cross and fade at every turn and it is pointless to try to define their exact nature. For the ambiguities are the whole meaning of the poem and the source of all its delight.

It is in this area that I think Scève was most interested and here that he expended most of his energies. What has generally appealed to modern critics, on the other hand, is Scève's use of imagery. This can, on occasion, be of the greatest interest, but a poem such as dizain 175 which I discussed earlier is in no way typical of the bulk of the poems in the *Délie*. In dizain 175 Scève attempts to convey an experience through a sustained use of imagery, but the majority of the dizains in his collection have

very little to do with imagery in any sense that a modern reader
understands the term. Look at dizain 248, for example:

> Ce mien languir multiplie la peine
> Du fort desir, dont tu tiens l'esperance,
> Mon ferme aymer t'en feit seure, & certaine,
> Par lon travail, qui donna l'asseurance.
>   Mais toy estant fiere de ma souffrance,
> Et qui la prens pour ton esbatement,
> Tu m'entretiens en ce contentement
> (Bien qu'il soit vain) par l'espoir, qui m'attire,
> Comme vivantz tout d'un sustantement
> Moy de t'aymer, & toy de mon martyre.[40]

Not only is this typical of a large number of poems in the *Délie*,
but the method is typical also of many poems which belong to
the courtly tradition. As Chamard comments: 'C'est le défaut
fréquent de la chanson courtoise, qu'au lieu de s'abandonner à la
passion, le poète raisonne sur elle et disserte subtilement sur ce
qu'il sent ou croit sentir.'[41] The approach in dizain 248 is a
totally abstract one and it is clear that the aim is to produce the
impression of a reasoned analysis, rather than to explore a
particular problem through the use of imagery. Saulnier, noting
the frequent appearance of words such as *esprit, âme, vertu,
affection, désir, volonté*, in the poetry of Pernette du Guillet,
concludes that, with a few exceptions: 'on ne trouvera dans
toute l'œuvre [of Pernette] que des évocations de sentiments et
d'idées.'[42] I think this tendency towards abstraction derives
directly from the way in which the courtly tradition developed
in France, and it often leads poets like Scève to indulge in an
over-subtle presentation and analysis of emotions. In dizain 248
we find the poet's beloved as ever in possession of the keys to
life and death. She is certain of his devotion and appears to take
a delight in his suffering, playing with his hopes to such an
extent that he can say she is living on his constant agonies in
exactly the same way that he lives on his love for her. The
argument is clear enough in outline and the final line is
obviously designed to make an impression on the reader, but the
effect is rather of an intellectual than a lyrical inspiration. The
long, four-syllable abstractions at the rhyme in lines six, seven,
and nine, have a displeasing effect on the modern ear; they are
paralleled, however, in numerous poems, both in the *Délie* and

elsewhere. Compare the following lines from the *Jardin*, for instance:

> . . . je choisy par vray assentement
> Une dame de tous biens acomplye
> A laquelle soubzmis entierement
> Corps, cueur et biens habandonneement.

[fo. xxvii]

I think there is a similar phenomenon at work in English poetry of the time. C. S. Lewis quotes the following lines from a sonnet by Thomas Wyatt, pointing out quite rightly that: 'No later sonneteer could learn anything from lines like

> Yet this trust I have of full great aperaunce
> Since that decept is aye retourneable
> Of very force it is aggreable
> And therewithal be done the recompense.'[43]

A. Glauser says: 'Pour exister, la poésie a besoin d'objets à contempler', and this is probably true for the modern reader, though not, I suspect, for Scève. Certainly the practice of accumulating unwieldy abstractions at the rhyme is something which was severely curtailed by Ronsard and du Bellay from the time of their earliest collections, and there is considerable significance in this development, as I shall hope to show later.

Because of Scève's apparent disposition towards abstract contemplation and intellectual formulations of sentiment, one finds numerous poems in the *Délie* which seem uneven in texture; poems which, as it were, share both in the tendency towards abstraction and in the desire to escape from it. Weber draws attention to this phenomenon, finding in some otherwise convincing poems 'une zone prosaïque où dominent l'effort de l'enchaînement logique et la subtilité du cliché pétrarquiste'.[44] P. Boutang makes a similar point and uses poems such as dizain 346 in illustration. The first six lines of this poem, he suggests, have no real poetic beauty:

> A si hault bien de tant saincte amytié
> Facilement te debvroit inciter,
> Sinon debvoir, ou honneste pitié,
> A tout le moins mon loyal persister,
> Pour unyment, & ensemble assister
> Lassus en paix en nostre eternel throsne.

The abstractions here combine to say very little that is arresting. Through the well-worn phrases like 'hault bien' or 'saincte amytié' and the traditional concepts of *debvoir* and *pitié*, Scève is formulating a mild reproach concerning his beloved's lack of interest in his passion. The sixth line suggests that the poet is talking about the future of their love in the life to come, but the way in which it is expressed is not particularly moving. The final four lines, however, are quite different, for Scève moves away from an abstract presentation towards one of the most memorable images in the *Délie*. The rivers Rhône and Saône meet at Lyon, Scève's native city, and he uses this geographical fact to illustrate the inevitability of love in death:

> N'apperçoy tu de l'Occident le Rhosne
> Se destourner, & vers Midy courir,
> Pour seulement se conjoindre a sa Saone
> Jusqu'a leur Mer, ou tous deux vont mourir?[45]

Boutang also discusses dizain 372, which has two fine opening and concluding lines, separated by the 'arides douceurs' of ll. 3–8. Scève wishes to say that Délie is at once the instigator of his passion and the means of controlling it, and he expresses this antithesis both in the traditional abstract way ('ton œil cruellement benin') and, much more interestingly, in terms of the image of the cedar, which was apparently used as an antidote to snake bites:

> Tu m'es le Cedre encontre le venin
> De ce Serpent en moy continuel . . .

The poet then moves on to make the traditional eulogy of the sweet breath and voice of his beloved, and once again he expresses this both in a conventional antithesis ('Celle doulceur celestement humaine') and through the image of the perfumes of Arabia, a comparison no less traditional, but far more effective in conveying the uniqueness of Délie's influence and one which frees the poem from the preceding abstractions:

> Alors qu'Amour par effect mutuel
> T'ouvre la bouche, & en tire a voix plaine
> Celle doulceur celestement humaine,
> Qui m'est souvent peu moins, que rigoureuse,
> Dont spire (ô Dieux) trop plus suave alaine,
> Que n'est Zephire en l'Arabie heureuse.

When Délie speaks the effect is softer than the passing of the
west wind over Arabia, the land of myrrh. But it is interesting
to note that Scève does not describe this event in
straightforward terms: Délie does not simply open her mouth
and speak. Her action is the result of the intervention of one of
the oldest and most commonly used abstract figures, *Amour*, a
figure that Scève invokes here, no doubt, without giving the
matter a second thought:

> Alors qu'Amour par effect mutuel
> T'ouvre la bouche . . .

This kind of distancing—or so I think it appears to a modern
reader—is very common in the *Délie*, and I shall explore the
question in more detail later. It is a technique which derives
from a very long tradition and I think it can be shown that, as
far as its use in lyric poetry is concerned, Scève stands almost at
the end of that tradition. If a reference to an abstract
intermediary is to carry conviction there must be a firm sense in
the reader's mind of a personalised figure lying behind the
abstraction; otherwise the effect is often tedious and one needs
to adopt an almost exclusively intellectual or analytical
approach to the elucidation of the poem in question.

The point is well illustrated by a comparison between dizains
129 and 148 of the *Délie*. I. D. McFarlane thinks it strange that
such poems as the former have not made much impression on
readers over the years, even though they display, on close
examination, considerable poetic merits. But dizain 129 is, I
think, a rather uneven poem, and it is its tendency towards
abstraction which is largely responsible for this. The opening
lines are attractive enough, and the final image may well be
arresting, but in between there is a large section in which Scève
relates his problem to the traditional pair of abstractions *ame* and
Corps in a way that is difficult to follow and not very rewarding
after the effort has been made:

> Le jour passé de ta doulce presence
> Fust un serain en hyver tenebreux,
> Qui fait prouver la nuict de ton absence
> A l'œil de l'ame estre un temps plus umbreux
> Que n'est au Corps ce mien vivre encombreux,
> Qui maintenant me fait de soy refus.
>   Car dès le poinct, que partie tu fus,

> Comme le Lievre accroppy en son giste,
> Je tendz l'oreille, oyant un bruyt confus,
> Tout esperdu aux tenebres d'Egypte.[46]

Dizain 148, on the other hand, is not uneven in this way, for throughout the poem Scève sustains a relationship between the emotions he feels and the state of the natural, visible world. The opening six lines are a conventional but convincing enough description of the passage from winter into spring:

> Voy que l'Hyver tremblant en son sejour,
> Aux champs tous nudz sont leurs arbres failliz.
> Puis le Printemps ramenant le beau jour,
> Leur sont bourgeons, fueilles, fleurs, fruictz sailliz:
>   Arbres, buissons, & hayes, & tailliz
> Se crespent lors en leur gaye verdure.

If the poem had nothing more to say than that it would be pretty and that is all. One expects a comparison with the state of the lover to follow this description of the state of nature and if this were done as conventionally as the opening of the dizain the whole effect would not be very memorable. But Scève builds on the conventional description and produces an analogy with his own state of mind that is extraordinarily original in the manner of its telling. He is indeed like the winter when his beloved is cold towards him and when she softens her attitude the change in him is just like a change in seasons: the theme may be banal, but the poetry is of the highest order:

>   Tant que sur moy le tien ingrat froit dure,
> Mon espoir est denué de son herbe:
> Puis retournant le doulx Ver sans froidure
> Mon An se frise en son Avril superbe.[47]

The argument is perfectly clear and there is no need for the poet to establish a formal link between the coming of spring and Délie's change of heart, in the way that winter is directly linked with her coldness. The final image is one that merits a good deal of attention for it is of the kind that seems to me unparalleled in earlier French love poetry, or indeed in any of the love poetry known to me before the nineteenth century. In comparison, some of Ronsard's most famous images can seem too neat and predictable. But I would stress once again that images such as one finds in dizain 148 are quite rare in the *Délie* as a whole, and that Scève has major preoccupations in areas that are unrelated to the general subject of imagery.

I should like to conclude this chapter with a word on the obscurity of the *Délie*. Much of the obscurity is in fact closely connected with the question of abstraction that we have been discussing, and, as Saulnier perceptively remarks, 'l'obscurité de Scève est en raison directe de la banalité', or at least this is frequently the case.[48] There are numerous poems in the *Délie* which, once one has disentangled them, reveal a disappointingly superficial attitude or argument. The impression that Scève's collection is not as straightforward as it might be is not one that is shared only by modern readers; the poem by Charles Fontaine which I quoted earlier demonstrates the point very well: everyone agrees, he says, that Scève's lines are so difficult to follow that 'ilz requierent un docteur' and it may well be that the extreme forms of abstraction which we find in the *Délie* were as much a problem for those outside Scève's immediate circle as they are for a reader today. There are, however, only a few poems in the *Délie* which are truly obscure in the grand manner and I give as an example dizain 331, perhaps the most famous of all the virtuoso pieces:

> L'humidité, Hydraule de mes yeulx,
> Vuyde tousjours par l'impie en l'oblique,
> L'y attrayant, pour air des vuydes lieux,
> Ces miens souspirs, qu'a suyvre elle s'applique.
>   Ainsi tous temps descent, monte, & replique,
> Pour abrever mes flammes appaisées.
>   Doncques me sont mes larmes si aisées
> A tant pleurer, que sans cesser distillent?
> Las du plus hault goutte a goutte elles filent,
> Tombant aux sains, dont elles sont puysées.[49]

I. D. McFarlane, following the lead given by the edition of Parturier, writes as follows in his notes on the poem: 'This dizain becomes clearer when one remembers the old theory about the physiology of tears. Tears were believed to well up from the heart, and then to pass through the eyes; they then fell upon the heart or chest, thus coming full circle.' So the poet compares the constant recirculation of his tears to the action of a water clock, and the cause of all the suffering is, as ever, Délie, the hard-hearted beloved. Now both Parturier and McFarlane see the movement of the poet's tears as being essentially a self-centred affair, the poet sobbing his heart out in isolation. But I think this is a misreading, and a rather amusing one at that. For the final line contains the plural form *sains* (= modern *seins*) and this is surely far more plausibly understood in relation to a woman than to a man. The old notion of a Platonic sequence dies hard. The poet in fact is not alone with his recirculating tears; he buries his face in the bosom of his beloved and his tears can thus quite naturally be said to circulate via her unreceptive body ('par l'impie'). Parturier quotes the following passage from Alberti in connection with dizain 331: 'Et le mie lagrime, cadendo nel seno, tornano onde furono premute, al core' ('And my tears, falling on to my breast, return to my heart, whence they were dispatched'), and if Scève really had this passage in mind, the shift from the singular *seno* to the plural *sains* would have been a fine ironic touch indeed.

I should now like to pass on to a discussion of possible Italian influences in the *Délie*, thus renewing the investigation into the transmission of themes and devices which I began in the first chapter of this book. In so doing it is all too easy to lose sight of some of the basic points we have made about the love poetry in the *Délie*, but the question of Petrarchism is clearly a complex one and I think one has inevitably to adopt a rather detailed, and at times rather dry, approach to the available material, if one is to provide a proper picture of the developments in French love poetry before the advent of the Pléiade.

3 'Petrarchism' and the *Délie*

If one poses the question: to what extent is the poetry of the
Délie dependent on Italian influences, I would answer
comparatively little. This reaction may seem surprising in view
of the vast amount of critical writing which has attempted to
place Scève firmly within an Italianate tradition of love poetry,
but it is not as indefensible as it may seem at first sight. V.-L.
Saulnier, writing in 1944, in an article on Pernette du Guillet, a
minor poetess who may well have been the chief inspiration
behind the *Délie*, discussed the various influences at work in her
poetry and concluded that 'la part de l'influence pétrarquiste est
mince à côté de l'ensemble des autres'; while in his main work
on Scève Saulnier says quite correctly that 'Ce qu'on nomme
trop souvent matière et manière pétrarquistes, ne sont que l'écho
d'une tradition composite', a point I have tried to underline
with reference to the poetry of Clément Marot.[1] J. B.
Wadsworth, in his edition of Champier's *Le Livre de vraye
amour*, notes how critics are often led astray in their attempt to
demonstrate the overwhelming 'Italianism' of Champier's
work, and elsewhere he also questions the common critical
assumption that Italianism implies 'something fresh, something
beautiful, in complete contrast with the old and worn-out'.[2] As
far as the *Délie* is concerned, I think it is possible to show that
Italian poetry has exercised only a superficial influence and that
it has little to do with the basic form and content of Scève's
verse.

How is one to define influence in the context of French
Renaissance love poetry? The problems are considerable, but I
think that stylistic as well as thematic criteria must enter into
one's deliberations. As I pointed out in my discussion of the
possible influence of Petrarchism on the poetry of Marot, the
mere presence of identical themes in the work of two poets does
not of itself justify the postulation of close relationships. As
Samuel Stern, the discoverer of the Romance *kharjas*, put it in
his discussion (and rejection) of possible Arabic influences on
troubadour poetry, 'nella storia le simiglianze non sempre

implicano rapporti', a good working motto for anyone interested in the love poetry of the Renaissance.³ Before I begin a more detailed consideration of the problems in respect of the *Délie*, I will give two brief examples to illustrate my approach to the subject in general. My first example concerns a possible linguistic borrowing from the Greek Anthology in the opening dizain of Scève's collection:

> Voicy (ô paour d'agreables terreurs)
> Mon Basilisque avec sa poingnant' veue
> Perçant Corps, Cœur, & Raison despourveue,
> Vint penetrer en l'Ame de mon Ame.

The phrase 'l'Ame de mon Ame' has received occasional critical comment to the effect that it rather successfully conveys an impression of love penetrating into the innermost depths of the poet's emotional centre. I am not sure myself that it works completely as a device, but it is interesting to note that there is an exact parallel in a poem by Meleager in the Greek Anthology:

> Ἐντὸς ἐμῆς κραδίης τὴν εὔλαλον Ἡλιοδώραν
> ψυχὴν τῆς ψυχῆς ἔπλασεν αὐτὸς Ἔρως.⁴

The Greek Anthology was first printed in Florence (1494), while the first edition of the Greek text to be published in France appeared in 1531. Scève could obviously have known the Meleager poem, though no one to my knowledge, and certainly not Hutton, has ever claimed that he did. In a case like this, and there are many similar examples of slight linguistic 'borrowings' in the *Délie*, I tend to conclude that the resemblances are probably fortuitous, though naturally one can never be sure. At least I think the reader should be on his guard to the fact that isolated linguistic parallels may mean absolutely nothing at all in terms of the possible influence of one poet on another. My second example concerns not a linguistic, but a thematic parallel, and involves the following lines from dizain 334 of the *Délie*:

> Mes larmes donc n'ont elles peu estaindre
> Mon feu, ou luy mes grandz pleurs dessecher?
> Non: mais me font, sans l'un l'aultre empecher,
> Comme boys vert, bruler, pleurer, & plaindre.

The discussion of these lines by Parturier, Weber, and McFarlane reveals the thematic school in full armour. Scève's lines contain two basic themes, that of the opposition of fire and water, and that of green wood sputtering within a fire. These two themes are also to be found in two unrelated strambotti by the Italian poet Serafino;[5] hence all three of the above critics maintain that here Scève has fused a couple of Italian poems and applied the material to his own ends. The location of Scève's 'source' also provides some scope for demonstrating that Scève has improved on his originals. But this is a very dangerous form of textual criticism. One may recall the example of the sonnet by Sir Thomas Wyatt beginning 'Like to these unmeasurable mountains': this used to be compared with a poem by Saint-Gelais ('Voyant ces monts de veue ainsi lointaine') and Wyatt's departures from the 'original' were held to constitute the essence of his own originality. Then it transpired that both Wyatt and Saint-Gelais had derived their sonnets from an Italian poem ascribed to Sannazaro ('Simile a questi smisurati monti'), and thereupon Wyatt's originality turned out to be simply a close adherence to the common source, rather than a daring deviation from the French. The case of dizain 334 of the *Délie* is yet more problematical, for it is not even possible to show that Scève had definitely read the two strambotti which are held to be his source. There are no linguistic parallels here between Scève and Serafino, simply a coincidence of themes which may be of no significance at all. The whole substance of Scève's lines is also to be found in Saint-Gelais, to go no further:

> Ce n'est poinct pleur, madame, qui me tient,
> C'est seullement qu'Amour m'a attisé
> Dedans son feu, et de la flamme vient
> Mon grant ennui! Comme j'ay advisé,
> Et comme on voyt qu'ung bois verd embrasé,
> Dedans ung feu, rend de l'eaue à grant force;
> Ainsi mon corps, lequel la flamme force,
> Gecte ceste eaue que vous appelez pleur.
> De résister à ce feu je n'ay force,
> Par quoy me fault endurer ma douleur.[6]

Stylistically Scève's lines are not close either to Serafino or to Saint-Gelais, and in this kind of situation I think it is pointless to look for a specific source; it is more fruitless still to assume one has found the only possible source and to proceed with one's critical commentaries on that basis.

Most Petrarchan criticism has been completely thematic as far as questions of influence are concerned. The term Petrarchism itself is frequently used as a critical shorthand, covering a whole range of vague connections between various poets. As H. Hauvette pointed out: 'traduire est une chose, imiter en est une autre, et puiser des inspirations, reproduire un certain tour de sensibilité ou même de forme, pour en faire de libres applications, en est une troisième.'[7] In common critical language the term Petrarchism is used to refer to both Petrarch himself and to numerous followers, self-declared or presumed, talented or otherwise; and beyond this the word is applied to evidence of direct translations, to close imitations, and to supposed vague reminiscences and the airiest notions of sympathy and affinity which may or may not have existed between the various poets concerned. It is true that some critics have tried to improve on this rather nebulous situation: L. Forster in his book *The Icy Fire* distinguishes between Petrarchan (with reference to Petrarch himself) and petrarchan (referring to the followers of Petrarch) and in this he is followed by D. G. Coleman in her work on Scève, entitled *Maurice Scève: Poet of Love—Tradition and Originality*. But I do not know whether this improves the situation greatly, and I have not found it profitable to maintain the same distinctions in the present work. The problems of definition are well illustrated by looking at Desonay's comments on Saulnier's perfectly accurate assessment, which I quoted at the beginning of this chapter, to the effect that Petrarchism is frequently used merely as a shorthand expression to denote the existence of a 'tradition composite':

Où nous ne suivons plus M. Saulnier, c'est quand il avance que 'ce qu'on nomme trop souvent matière et manière pétrarquistes, ne sont que l'écho d'une tradition composite'; et d'alléguer l'*Anthologie grecque*, les érotiques latins, comme Ovide, Catulle, voire nos romanciers courtois. L'erreur consiste à voir dans le 'glukupikron' [i.e. the Greek γλυκύπικρον 'bitter-sweet', first used to describe the effects of love by Sappho, as far as I know] et le procédé antithétique, en général, l'essence même du pétrarquisme. Il y a bien autre chose, aux pages des *Rime* [i.e. the *Canzoniere*] et des *Trionfi*, que ces développements stéréotypés sur les thèmes: 'chose amère-miel', 'froid-chaud', 'bas-haut', etc. . . . Le sentiment

de l' écoulement de toute chose vivante, voilà le grand thème
pétrarquien . . . aucun écrivain antérieur n'a inventé, pour rendre la
fuite du temps, des images aussi concrètes que Pétrarque . . .[8]

Both Desonay and Saulnier are quite correct in what they have
to say: they are simply talking about different things, though
under the same general heading 'Petrarchism'. Saulnier is
referring to Petrarchism as a general force in literature, while
Desonay is talking about the inimitable qualities of Petrarch, the
individual poet. Of course there is a great deal in the *Canzoniere*
which is not dependent on the technique of the antithesis, but so
far as the succeeding Petrarchan tradition was concerned it was
precisely the stereotypes like the antithesis which were most
easily imitable, not the greater example of Petrarch's ability to
convey an individual emotional response to a perennial human
predicament.

    Thus one begins with a problem of definition: what are we to
take the term Petrarchism to mean, in the context of French
Renaissance love poetry? I think it is fundamentally a question
of prestige. French poets were above all inspired by Petrarch's
example and derived from him the impulse and in some sense
the confidence to achieve what he had already achieved for the
Italian poetic tradition. This does not necessarily mean that a
French poet anxious to make a name for himself would have
undertaken a close study of Petrarch's work or of the work of
Petrarch's Italian followers. You might easily have sailed under
a Petrarchan flag with little direct knowledge of the master, just
as today some follow Marx without any knowledge of the
master at all. Such an approach to French Renaissance
Petrarchism would free the critic from the laborious search for
sources that has dominated much discussion of sixteenth-century
love poetry. Saulnier and Desonay are, on this point, in
complete agreement. The former writes of Maurice Scève: 'Ce
qu'il prit vraiment à Pétrarque, c'est le dessein d' écrire un
canzoniere', while the latter says of Ronsard: 'La leçon de
Pétrarque . . . n'est pas tant de fournir un répertoire
d'expressions et d'images que de communiquer . . . le sens du
"pouvoir formel de l'art"', and in this connection Desonay
rightly points to the minimal value of a number of textual
parallels which Laumonier has drawn between Petrarch and
Ronsard.[9] To go beyond the position which I have outlined here

is to involve oneself in some extremly complex problems, as I.
Murray makes clear:

> Unquestionable ascriptions of 'influence' can very seldom be made:
> they cannot be dogmatic unless there is a strong verbal echo, and a
> strong verbal echo really only proves itself, and not the thought
> behind it. If we have evidence of exactly what an author read, if he
> did not read too much, and if he had a verbal memory, influence is
> fairly easy to ascertain, and of little importance. Influence in the
> shape of ideas is something infinitely more difficult to trace, and
> very dangerous to dogmatize about.[10]

I think if one is prepared to accept the force of these arguments
then much that is complex about Petrarchism becomes quite
simple. The question of the chronology of Petrarchan influence
in France is a case in point. It is not, I think, a question that
could ever be satisfactorily resolved because there will never be
agreement about what one is discussing. If one can accept that
Petrarchism is basically a gradually developing sense of the
prestige of the Italian poetic tradition, then one will not worry
very much about the precise chronology. As it is the situation is
a totally confused one. C. A. Mayer has attempted to situate the
beginnings of French Petrarchism at some point before 1527. J.
Aynard, writing of Italian influence in Lyon, claimed that
'Intellectuellement, l'influence italienne est . . . plus tardive
qu'on ne le dit généralement', and pointed to the 1540s as the
period of real importance in this respect.[11] Saulnier, finding a
need to define the indefinable, provides what seem to me to be
two mutually contradictory statements: for at one point he
writes, 'Le pétrarquisme ne sera que vers 1550 l'objet d'un
engouement véritable', while earlier in the same book he had
written, 'c'est vers 1537 que commence, pour les Pétrarquistes,
et surtout pour Pétrarque personnellement, l'heure de la plus
grande gloire'.[12] I. D. McFarlane, while agreeing with the
former quotation, suggests that the term 'Italianism' be
substituted for the term 'Petrarchism'. This is a welcome idea,
insofar as a number of French poets, including Scève, were
clearly acquainted with Italian writers who do not fall within
the conventional category of Petrarchan poets, but I do not
think that a change in nomenclature can alter the material
problems of definition that are posed by the search for a strict
chronology.

I suppose it is clear from what I have written thus far that I would rather avoid the use of the term Petrarchism altogether. To suggest, as I. D. McFarlane does, that 'The *Délie* rests on a foundation of Petrarchism' (p. 28) serves merely to underline a common critical approach without attempting to analyse the preconceptions which lie behind it. The work of C. A. Mayer on Marot seems to me to highlight the dangers of relying too heavily on shorthand notations and this forces one to look again at the whole range of critical writing that has been devoted to the fortunes of the Petrarchan tradition in France. There used to be a view that Petrarchism in France was linked with the military exploits of Charles VIII (king of France from 1483 to 1498, and conqueror of the kingdom of Naples in 1495), but this has long since been abandoned as too simplistic, rather like the notion that the French Renaissance begins in 1500. In its place there has developed what I see as the correct view of Petrarchism as a force which evolved very gradually in France and whose fortunes are traced by F. Simone in his book *Il rinascimento francese*. Petrarch first arrived in Avignon in 1326 and Simone suggests that from that time onwards, and all through the fifteenth century, there was a growing interest in Petrarch as a moral philospher, but little interest in him as a vernacular poet. Then, at the end of the fifteenth century, the French public began to show greater favour to the vernacular works, which affected initially only the fortunes of the *Trionfi* but which later spread to include the *Canzoniere* also. Simone considers that the original impulse to discover the *Trionfi* sprang from a continuing interest in Petrarch as a philosopher, rather than a poet, and he sees the aim of the first French translation of the *Trionfi* (by Georges de la Forge, in 1514) as being essentially moralistic. This kind of approach on the part of the French reading public would account for the fact that an interest in the *Canzoniere* developed only very slowly: Vasquin Philieul's complete translation of the work appeared at the surprisingly late date of 1555 (in *Toutes les euvres vulgaires de Françoys Pétrarque*). As soon as one attempts to move away from this very general evolutionary view, however, the picture becomes immediately much more obscure. As with the question of the chronology of Petrarchism in France, so with the question of the kind of Petrarchism which French poets are supposed to have followed: as soon as you attempt to be precise the insoluble problems of definition reappear. For Vianey, the chief influence on French poets in the earlier sixteenth century derived, not from Petrarch himself, but from the Italian followers of Petrarch: 'Nos poètes imitèrent, non Pétrarque lui-même—quand un peuple s'engoue d'une littérature moderne se met-il à l'école d'écrivains morts depuis tant d'années?—mais les pétrarquistes italiens de leur temps.'[13] Hauvette followed more or less the same line in his *Les Poésies lyriques de Pétrarque*, though he considered that Vianey had failed to deal adequately with the obvious evidence of first-hand knowledge of Petrarch that is revealed, for example, in the translations of Marot and Peletier du Mans. Saulnier in his turn reacted completely against the views of Vianey, claiming that they were much too exclusive: 'Dans la mesure où les poètes du doux-amer s'inscrivent dans le sillage particulier des Italiens, on ne voit pas que Pétrarque ait jamais été éclipsé comme modèle par ses émules italiens.'[14] While C. Pellegrini noted with symbolic satisfaction that when Charles VIII passed through Florence in 1494, on his way to conquer the kingdom of Naples, he was presented with a manuscript of Petrarch's *Trionfi*.[15]

The disagreements over the form of Petrarchism which was taken into French poetry seem to me inevitable in the nature of things. There is so little contemporary evidence to justify one point of view or another, and the whole question thus remains largely subjective. Consider some of the references to Petrarch in the poetry of early sixteenth-century France: they tell us almost nothing about any direct relationships which may have existed between French and Italian literature; there is nothing that could not have derived from simple hearsay. Jean Lemaire wrote the following lines in 1513:

> Je feis maint vers, maint couplet, et maint metre,
> Cuydant suivir, par noble Poësie,
> Le bon Petrarque, en amours le vray maistre.[16]

While two years later, Clément Marot refers to Petrarch in these lines:

> Ovidius, maistre Alain Charetier,
> Pétrarque, aussi le *Rommant de la Roze*,
> Sont les messez, le bréviaire et psaultier
> Qu'en celuy temple on dit en ryme et prose.[17]

In 1533, Pierre Grognet praises Petrarch as a 'bon facteur, vulgaire et latin' and also comments, in a scarcely inspired way, on Serafino:

Seraphin natif d'Ytalie
Estoit de bonne poesie.[18]

And there are numerous similar references in poetry of the time, none of them to my knowledge any more instructive. This is true of the situation as late as 1549; for of the five references to Petrarch in du Bellay's *Deffence et illustration de la langue françoyse*, E. H. Wilkins selects as the most notable the following: 'Pour le sonnet donques tu as Petrarque & quelques modernes Italiens' (bk. II, iv).[19] It should be recognised that a reference to Petrarch's name means nothing by itself; we should remember after all that the name of Homer was long repeated as a model of literary excellence by people who could never have read a word of the *Iliad* or the *Odyssey*. So with Petrarch too, I am sure there must always have been many in the sixteenth century as now who knew him 'de nom seulement',[20] and this situation is undoubtedly the same where Petrarch's Italian followers are concerned. At what is generally considered to be the time of enormous Bembist influence on French love poetry, Peletier du Mans in his *Art Poëtique* of 1555 readily admits that he has never read a word of Bembo's poetry: 'On tient . . . que Bembe an à fet [i.e. has written sonnets] d'aussi sublimes que les siens [i.e. Petrarch's]: Mes je confesse ne les avoer vùz.'[21]

Critical writing about Italian literature in France becomes much more interesting in the second half of the sixteenth century than it had been in the earlier period, even though it is full of inaccuracies of one kind or another. Many of these inaccuracies derive from patriotic zeal, an attempt to highlight the French tradition at the expense of the Italian, a point which has made me think long and hard in case I have fallen into the same kind of error in the present book. Both Claude Fauchet, in his *Recueil de l'origine de la langue et poésie française* of 1581, and Henri Estienne, in his *De la precellence du langage françois* of 1579, claim that the French invented the sonnet, confusing the old Romance word *sonnet/sonet* which occurs in Old French and Occitanian (= 'music', 'song', poem', 'melody') with the specialised Italian use of the term to describe the fourteen-line poem. I think the confusion, though patriotically inspired, may well be a genuine one; Fauchet writes as follows:

> Et qui voudra fueilleter nos vieils Poetes, il trouvera dedans, les mots dont les Italiens se parent le plus: voire les noms & differences de leurs Rymes, Sonnets, Ballades, Lais, & autres. Quant au Sonnet, Guillaume de Lorris monstre que les François en ont usé: puis qu'il dit au Roman de la Rose, 'Lais d'Amours & Sonnets courtois.' [line 703][22]

While Estienne, in the preface to his book, says that French has two rivals, Italian and Spanish, of which Italian is by far the stronger; and he claims that he has toned down his criticism of the Italians, '& n'ay pas faict du pis que j'ay pu (car je leur pouvois oster l'honneur de ce mot aussi *Sonnetto*, & dire que nous avions *Sonnet* avant qu'eux eussent *Sonnetto*: voire objecter que Petrarque a pris quelques inventions de nos poetes Provençaux').[23]

Of course what Estienne says here is in some measure correct; the Italian *sonnetto* does derive etymologically from the Occitanian *sonet* and Petrarch was indeed acquainted with Occitanian lyric poetry—he called the troubadour Arnaut Daniel (fl. 1180–1200) 'gran maestro d'amor', a judgement which was also that of Dante. But the use of the word *sonnet* in French to describe the fourteen-line poem which had been invented by the Italians dates only from 1537, when it was employed in a translation of Castiglione's *Cortegiano*. Fauchet, a passionate defender of Old French texts, goes further astray than Estienne, for he seeks to reduce not only the importance of the Italian tradition, but also of the Occitanian, and he writes:

> Si Petrarque & ses semblables se sont aidez des plus beaux traits des chansons de Thiebaut Roy de Navarre, Gaces Brulez, Le Chastelain de Coucy, & autres anciens poetes François, que feront ceux qui vivent maintenant, quand ils viendront a fueilleter les œuvres de tant d'excellents poetes, qui sont venus depuis le regne du Roy François premier de ce nom?[24]

Fauchet has a wonderful sense of a literary tradition; he knows the names of the great trouvères of northern France, and has read much of their work—forty-nine poems by Gace Brulé, for example. But he is almost certainly wrong in ascribing trouvère influence to the poetry of Petrarch.

These later sixteenth-century comments, with their often

pronounced anti-Italian bias, belong to a very different climate from that in which the *Délie* was produced. Scève's collection of poems was superficially touched by the growing Italian fashion in France, but its roots lie deep in the French tradition. Look at the concluding line of the sixth dizain, for example:

En sa beaulté gist ma mort, & ma vie.

Lines such as these abound throughout the history of French love poetry. In Gace Brulé:

. . . en ma dame est et ma mort et ma vie.[25]

In Guillaume de Machaut:

Et quant en vous gist ma mort et ma vie.[26]

Or in the ballade inserted into the 1525 Lyon edition of the *Jardin*, which has as its refrain:

En elle gist ma vie et mon trespas.[27]

Wherever one looks in the *Délie* the problems of 'sources', themes and traditions are enormously complex, and I do not think they can be resolved simply by appealing to the ghost of Petrarch. The 1916 edition of the *Délie* by Parturier has achieved almost a critical notoriety for the wealth of its parallels between Scève and the Italians: Serafino, Petrarch, Bembo, Chariteo, Tebaldeo, Sassoferrato, and numerous others appear throughout this edition, and Parturier has often been taken to task for failing to respond to the poetic qualities of Scève's work. The latest critical edition of the *Délie* by I. D. McFarlane, although in part a conscious reaction against the Petrarchan excesses of Parturier, still insists on a number of parallels between the *Délie* and a variety of Italian poets, and I shall discuss the significance of some of these later in this chapter. Before that, however, I would like to examine the way in which the poetic climate in France had changed between the time of the Marot poems which I discussed in the first chapter of this book, that is the 1520s, and the period in which the *Délie* was mainly composed, the 1530s and early 1540s.

In general the change is a very slight one, though I think one can detect a growing interest in Italian poetry amongst some sections of the French literary community. From the mid 1530s onwards there is plenty of evidence of direct knowledge of the

Italian Petrarchans in the form of translations, though as we
have seen the fashion for translating began very early in the
sixteenth century and it did not necessarily have any effect on
the fortunes of the native French lyric. In 1534 Clément Marot's
translation of Petrarch's canzone *Standomi un giorno solo a la
fenestra* appeared and in 1544 his translation of six Petrarch
sonnets. The translation of the canzone was incorporated, with
due acknowledgement, into the complete translation of the
Canzoniere which Vasquin Philieul brought out in 1555. Marot's
rendering of this poem has been criticised, but it seems reasonable enough to me, and in any case Petrarch's original is
composed of a series of allegorical visions of Laura which are of
debatable interest for the modern reader. Peletier du Mans translated eleven of Petrarch's sonnets for his *Œuvres Poétiques* of 1547,
while C. Ruutz-Rees refers to a translation and a paraphrase of
Petrarch in Hugues Salel's *Œuvres* of 1540.[28] The first French
poem which derives directly from a Petrarch sonnet appeared in
1538, in the *Petit Oeuvre d'amour, et gaige d'amytié*; this *Dizain de
Pétrarque* is no more of a revelation than any of the other
Petrarchan exercises we have mentioned. As Françon puts it: 'il
est évident que notre dizain est plus fidèle à la tradition
française, qui nous a valu la ballade, "des contraires" de Villon,
qu'à la pensée de Pétrarque.'[29] The poem reads as follows:

> Ne trouvant paix homme ne me faict guerre
> J'espere et crains, ardant plus froid que glace
> Estant au ciel je ne bouge de terre.
> Rien je n'estrains et tout le monde embrasse
> Brief tous les jours vivant meurs et trespasse
> Prisonnier suis sans captif estre en serre
> J'ayme la paix, et ne la vueil requerre,
> Sans yeulx voy cler, et sans voix jecte cris
> Estant obscur suis plus luysant que verre,
> Et en douleur je trouve bien et ris.[30]

This already seems tired and lifeless, an imitation of that which
is most imitable in Petrarch, and I suspect the French translator
did not really understand the first line of the Italian original:

> Pace non trovo e non ò da far guerra,
> e temo e spero, et ardo e son un ghiaccio,
> e volo sopra 'l cielo e giaccio in terra,
> e nulla stringo e tutto 'l mondo abbraccio . . .[31]

It is so predictable that Petrarch's sonnet should have been turned into a French dizain.

I think the Italian fashion in France is in the early stages a largely aristocratic one, and it is partly for this reason that Scève's *Délie* is relatively untouched by it. Mellin de Saint-Gelais (1487–1558) was long ago credited by M. Piéri with having revealed Petrarch to the French, and if you do require that kind of chronological precision his name is as good as any; at least he is the right *sort* of poet for these purposes. He spent a long time in Italy and was later keeper of the royal library at Fontainebleau; his influence operated largely on a personal basis and A. H. Schutz, in his researches into the vernacular books held in Parisian private libraries of the sixteenth century, notes that 'in all our inventories there is not an entry of Mellin's poems, except for a Valois library which was not of the bourgeois type'.[32] Mellin de Saint-Gelais was in every sense a court poet: as D. Heartz explains, he followed the practice of Serafino and 'put his verses to music, sang them himself to the accompaniment of the lute, and was careful never to publish them, so that they might pass continually for improvisations' and Heartz points out too that the *Saingelais* which appeared in Lyon in 1547 was published without the author's consent.[33] Vianey suggested in 1909 that Saint-Gelais had wished to make himself the Serafino of France, and he detailed a number of direct translations that Saint-Gelais made of Italian poets: from Serafino, Philoxeno, Burchiello, Ariosto, Francesco Berni, and Sannazaro.[34] Saint-Gelais is at the same time in the vanguard of that reaction against the excesses of Italian lyricism that is usually called anti-Petrarchism, and I think that both Petrarchism and the reaction against it are best understood as fashions first of all and only secondarily as literary fashions. That is to say, there is in both a considerable element of posing, and that is why the learned search for sources seems so often misplaced. If you wanted to play the fashionable Italianate lover, or if you wanted to attack him, you picked up the superficial tricks of imagery, but you did not spend months in seclusion pouring over endless editions of Italian poets. Consider the following lines from a poem by Saint-Gelais which first appeared in the 1546 Paris edition of the *Rymes* of Pernette du Guillet—the poem is entitled *Autre epistre à une dame qui se plaignoit de n'avoir esté assez louée par M.D.S.G.* [= Mellin de Saint-Gelais] and the poet

makes it clear that any woman who is in need of an excessive
amount of praise would do well to search abroad:

> Je laisse faire à ces Italiens,
> Ou Espagnolz, tomber en voz liens,
> Qui disent plus qu'onques ilz ne penserent,
> Pour avoir mieux encores qu'ilz n'esperent.

The whole poem is sixty-six lines in length and has been
considered a forerunner of du Bellay's poem *A une dame* of 1553,
later entitled *Contre les Pétrarquistes*. What will the sly Spaniards
and Italians provide for a young woman who is not satisfied
with the compliments of her native land? The list turns out to be
endless:

> Ceulx là diront que les traitz de voz yeux
> Font devenir le Soleil envieux,
> Et que ce sont deux astres reluysants . . .
> Ilz vous diront que d'un ris seulement
> Vous eschauffez le plus froid element:
> Et que les biens, dont Arabie est pleine
> N'approchent point de vostre douce aleine.
> Ilz jureront que voz mains sont d'yvoire,
> Et que la neige aupres de vous est noire.
> Vos blanches dents, ou plustost Dyamants
> Sont la prison des espritz des amants:
> Et le Courail ou elles sont encloses
> Palist le taint des plus vermeilles roses . . .[35]

These lines seem to me to betray the presence of a new source of
inspiration in French poetry in a way revealed by none of the
other poems I have discussed so far, and certainly by none of the
translations from Italian. Though Saint-Gelais is making fun of
Petrarchism, he is playing with its images of praise in a sustained
manner and this is highly significant. For, as Forster says, 'praise
of the lady, however indirect, is the basic subject matter of
petrarchistic poetry, as it was for Petrarch himself'.[36] All
through the fifteenth century and right into the 1530s and 1540s
we find in France that deathless brand of abstract love poetry
that could have been written by anyone at any time. The
following lines from Jacques Moderne's collection *Le Parangon
des chansons*, a ten-volume work published in Lyon between
1538 and 1541, could belong as easily to the *Délie* as to the world
of the *Jardin de plaisance*:

Plus loing j'en suys, plus pres d'elle me sens
Si seul ne suys que sans elle puisse estre
Ne la voyant si bien se faict congnoistre
Que d'elle absent, absent ne me consens . . .[37]

Not an image to be found; it is scarcely any wonder that
women should have preferred to be praised in the Italian
manner—however superficial the new world might be, it was
infinitely more exciting and more feminine than the old.

It would be absurd to attempt to trace the sources of the
images in Saint-Gelais's poem: it is the fashion that counts
before everything else. Of course, Saint-Gelais also wrote
extensively in what I might now call the 'old style' and there is
nothing surprising about that:

Si la beauté qui vous rend si aimable,
N'estoit pareille à mon affection,
Elle seroit incertaine et muable,
Et je serois hors de subjection;
Mais comme seule elle a perfection,
Aussi parfaicte est ma vive estincelle.
L'une est céleste, et l'autre est éternelle,
L'une est sans feu, l'autre sans cruauté:
Telle beauté fait l'amour estre belle,
Et tel amour aimable la beauté.[38]

Once again one finds not a single image and indeed I think it is
only with the advent of the Pléiade that the Petrarchan images
of praise are properly acclimatised in France. Weber notes a few
expressions of praise in the *Délie* which are not to be found in
the work of Marot, but which reappear with the Pléiade, such
as the references to the 'mains yvoirines' in dizain 235 or the
'sourcilz Hebenins' of dizain 270.[39] But expressions like these are
the exception rather than the rule in the *Délie*, and that is why a
poem like dizain 235 stands out very clearly from the majority
of the poems in the collection:

Aumoins toy, clere, & heureuse fontaine,
Et vous, ô eaux fraisches, & argentines,
Quand celle en vous (de tout vice loingtaine)
Se vient laver ses deux mains yvoirines,
Ses deux Soleilz, ses levres corallines,
De Dieu créez pour ce Monde honnorer,

Debvriez garder pour plus vous decorer
L'image d'elle en voz liqueurs profondes.
    Car plus souvent je viendroys adorer
Le sainct miroir de voz sacrées undes.

This is, I think, the most 'Petrarchan' poem in the *Délie*. It is
concrete and visual in its praises, and above all there is a
sustained approach to its imagery. The sensuous, slightly
precious, description of a natural scene is totally clear, and any
delight which a reader may experience derives from his ability
to see himself as a part of that natural scene, rather than from an
intellectual capacity to think his way back along some abstract
argument. Dizain 235 is already in the world of the Pléiade:

Ell' prist son teint des beaux lyz blanchissans,
Son chef de l'or, ses deux levres des rozes,
Et du soleil ses yeux resplandissans . . .

[*Olive*, II]

And this is a world which is quite alien to the French tradition
as we have been discussing it so far, a tradition to which Scève
quite happily belongs in so far as the majority of the poems in
the *Délie* are concerned. Look at the opening of dizain 7, for
example, where the art is consciously verbal and not visual:

Celle beaulté, qui embellit le Monde
Quand nasquit celle en qui mourant je vis,
A imprimé en ma lumière ronde
Non seulement ses lineamentz vifz:
Mais tellement tient mes espritz raviz,
En admirant sa mirable merveille . . .[40]

Or consider the opening of dizain 12, where Scève has a single
line in the style of dizain 235, and then proceeds in a typically
abstract manner:

Ce lyen d'or, raiz de toy mon Soleil,
Qui par le bras t'asservit Ame, & vie,
Detient si fort avec la veue l'œil,
Que ma pensée il t'à toute ravie,
Me demonstrant, certes, qu'il me convie
A me stiller tout soubz ton habitude.[41]

I shall return to the whole question of abstraction and the *Délie*
in the following chapter of this book.

The most important general conclusion about Italianism and the *Délie* which one would make on the basis of Parturier's edition is that Scève appears to have been acquainted with a very large number of Italian writers, but that there are few positive linguistic borrowings from them in the collection as a whole. The Petrarchan influence on Scève would seem to be essentially a matter of thematic resemblances, of a vague sense of affinity, and this situation raises the same sort of problems as we encountered in dealing with the rondeaux of Marot. I know that Renaisance man, fresh with enthusiasm from the invention of the printing press, was supposed to have been a voracious reader, but could Scève really have read the works of Tebaldeo, Petrarch, Serafino, Speroni, Sannazaro, Sasso, Sassoferrato, Poliziano, Martelli, Lorenzo de Medici, Ebreo, Chariteo, Britonio, Bembo and the rest, and then absorbed the 'Italian spirit' so completely by the time the *Délie* was published in 1544 that his work could be described as a Petrarchan sequence? Ultimately any judgement will be a very subjective one, but it may be as well to review the few available facts that are of relevance in this case. Certainly it is true that little Italian poetry had been published in France by 1544. There seems to have been a single edition of Petrarch's vernacular poetry, the Lyon counterfeit of the famous 1501 Aldine edition published by Bembo, while Luigi Alamanni, an Italian poet who was resident at the French court for some years, brought out his *Opere toscane* in Lyon in 1532–33. Similarly, there had been very little Italian literature in French translation published by 1544, though we have already mentioned the 1537 translation of Castiglione's *Cortegiano*: this was made by Jacques Colin and also appeared first in Lyon. After the date of publication of the *Délie* the situation changes quite markedly. There are editions of Petrarch's Italian poetry published in France in 1545, 1550, 1551, 1558, 1564, and 1574, while Bembo's *Asolani* were translated into French in 1545. The 1545 Lyon edition of Petrarch's work has always been of interest to readers of Scève, for it carries the following dedication: 'A non men virtuoso, che dotto M. Mauritio Scæva, Giovan di Tournes [an italianised form of the publisher's name, Jean de Tournes] suo affettionatissimo, s.' There is also a 1547 edition of Dante's *Divina Commedia* from the same publisher with the dedication: 'Al molto ingenioso et dotto, M. Mauritio Sceva.'[42] But fascinating as these details are, they should not lead one to ignore the fact that the publishing situation in France in the first half of the sixteenth century was very little different from that in the closing years of the fifteenth century, as it emerges from Brunet's *La France littéraire au XVe siècle*. Brunet demonstrates the great popular appeal exercised by the Romances of Chivalry in France and by contemporary French poetry, while McFarlane points out that the popularity of the Rhétoriqueurs was maintained at least until the 1530s. In the world of music one notes a similar situation. G. Dottin, writing with reference to the age of Marot, stresses the fact that 'Le public d'alors, s'il réclame sans cesse des chansons "nouvelles" . . . n'en reste pas moins attaché aux strophes et aux airs favoris de la génération de Louis XII' (king of France from 1498 to 1515), and that 'la cour de François I connaît un renouveau de l'ancien Amour courtois, d'expression strictement traditionnelle (au moins jusque vers 1540)'.[43] The state of the musical world also helps one to remember that influences do not always operate in one direction only: 'During the first third of the century of the Renaissance, the stream of influence ran definitely from France into Italy . . . the Parisian *chanson* invaded the peninsula and penetrated it at the same time as did the troops of Francis I.'[44] Attaingnant, the most famous of the music publishers, 'went through six active years and approximately fifty collections before printing some pieces with texts in Italian . . . in all [there were] five Italian-texted pieces printed in Paris in the first half of the century, out of a total of about 2,000 chansons'. While the Lyon music publisher Jacques Moderne, Italian by origin, included only six pieces with Italian texts in all the volumes of his *Parangon des chansons*, published between 1538 and 1541.[45]

✗ Of course the fact that there was a flourishing French tradition in poetry and music all through the 1530s and that very little Italian work had been published in France by 1544 is by no means conclusive in establishing the context in which Scève may have been working. He may have had access to any of the numerous collections of poetry that were being published in Italy during the early years of the sixteenth century, and indeed it is usually assumed that whatever was available in Italy would have been almost immediately available in Lyon, given the favourable geographical circumstances. Certainly the popularity of the Italian Petrarchists in their homeland is not open to

question, nor is that of Petrarch himself. In fact there were 140
editions of Petrarch's works published in Italy in the sixteenth
century, of which almost half appeared between 1537 and 1565.
Now, as far as Scève is concerned, there is some dispute among
critics as to whether he was most influenced by Petrarch himself
or by the Italian followers of Petrarch, of whom Serafino
Aquilano (1466–1500) is usually considered of greatest
importance in this respect. There are in fact as many forms of
Petrarchism as there are Petrarchist poets, but conventionally
one says that writers such as Serafino developed what was most
artificial and bizarre in the poetry of Petrarch, whereas Pietro
Bembo (1470–1547) attempted to restore Petrarchan poetry to
its original classical simplicity and purity. Like all such
generalisations, this one is in need of some qualification.
Serafino could indeed write in an extravagant style: look, for
example, at the sonnet beginning 'So che gran miraviglia al cor
ti prese'. Here the poet, having been struck by a thunderbolt,
appears encircled by flames before his beloved; however, he
explains that his body has not suffered any harm since, as his life
belongs totally to his lady, it was literally absent from him at the
time of the catastrophe. But it would be a mistake to assume that
all Serafino's verse is as extravagantly conceived as this. When
he writes in the 'excessive' style it is not because he cannot do
anything else; it is simply an attempt to entertain and to amuse,
and if we are to believe his biographer he was able to do this
with the greatest distinction. Whatever qualifications one may
wish to make, however, the fact remains that the publication of
Bembo's *Rime* in 1530 was an event of considerable importance
in the history of Italian Petrarchism and it raises some interesting
questions for those who see Scève as a writer who was in close
touch with the Italian literary tradition. No one has ever
suggested that the *Délie* is much influenced by Bembo. And so,
if Scève does indeed owe a great debt to Petrarch, he must have
made his discoveries in ignorance of Bembo's contributions in
this field, or else he must have chosen deliberately to ignore
them. If, on the other hand, Scève owes most to poets such as
Serafino, then we must assume that he either deliberately
followed a style he knew to be on the decline or that the Italian
fashion in Lyon lagged behind developments in Italy itself.
Whichever of these approaches one wishes to take, it will be
evident that a considerable number of problems are involved,

problems which disappear immediately if one accepts that
Italianism may not, after all, have been of such crucial
importance for the development of the *Délie*.

It is interesting to note in this connection that the traditional
view of Lyon as some sort of Italian colony has been challenged
in an article by M. Dassonville, published in 1965. He writes of
the Italian 'invasion' of Lyon in the following terms: 'Il n'est pas
douteux que la bourgeoisie et la "marchandise" lyonnaises
n'aient constaté, avec un mécontentement croissant, cette
invasion étrangère ... Il n'est pas moins douteux que les cercles
mondains et lettrés n'aient eu conscience de leur originalité, de
leur indépendance à l'égard de l'Italie autant que de Paris.'[46]
There was certainly a growing interest in Lyon in all things
Italian. The publisher Jean de Tournes writes of his work on the
edition of Alamanni's *Opere toscane* already mentioned, 'la qual
cosa mi mosse non solamente ad aprezar, ma ancora ad amar, e a
compiacermi molto in questa lingua toscana, di modo qu'alhora
dissegnai di continuar in questo volgare, como le mie facultà vi
si offeriranno.' And in 1551 we find Jean de Vauzelles writing to
Pietro Aretino about the *Délie* in the following terms:

> E se voi intendesti così la lingua nostra com' io la vostra, vi
> manderei alcune rime d'un mio fratello fatte in lode di una sua
> Delia, accompagnate di più propi e spirituali emblemi di quelli di
> Alciato ... Ma, perchè le rime nostre sono assai difficile a chi non
> le ha usate, non mi sono altramente disposto a mandarvene, bench'
> io non dubito che le giudicaresti degne d'esser italiane per più
> gratia.[47]

But though we have evidence of this developing interest in
Franco-Italian contacts, there is no reason to suppose that an
Italian invasion of Lyon killed off the native tradition in poetry
overnight. Certainly the reputation of Italian literature in Lyon
is high, at least by 1551, and I have no doubt that Scève would
have been happy to see his *Délie* discussed in the same terms as
Petrarch's *Canzoniere*, but this does not prove that the Italian
fashion in Lyon was anything more than a superficial
excitement. I am sure that there were exchanges of one kind or
another on various levels of economic, social, and poetic
activity, but the *Délie* does not, I think, demonstrate that these
exchanges had radically affected the cultural traditions of Lyon
by 1544.

Why, after all, should Scève have been drawn to such poets as Serafino, Chariteo, and Tebaldeo? The reputations of such men were dependent on personal factors that can have had no relevance for a poet writing outside Italy. Serafino, for example, had died forty-four years before the *Délie* was published. He was evidently a man of powerful character, a lover of many women, according to his biographer Vincentio Calmeta, whose *Vita del facondo poeta vulgare Seraphino Aquilano* first appeared in 1504, and a man who desired above all else to achieve fame and popularity during his own lifetime.[48] He managed to fall in love with a woman called Laura (described as being 'di mediocre honestà'), and he early on set himself to study Petrarch's vernacular works, 'li quali non solo hebbe familiarissimi, ma tanto bene con la musica li accordava che a sentirli da lui cantare nel liuto ogni altra harmonia superavano'.[49] After Serafino's death Francesco Flavio gathered together 'li sparsi membri del lacerato Seraphino' and this first edition of his poetry appeared in 1502. He remained enormously popular for some years, and one notes a concentration of editions of his work between 1502 and about 1517, the succeeding thirty-five years producing less than half the volume of these fifteen years just after his death. Chariteo, on the other hand, never seems to have been particularly popular at any stage. He died in 1514 and there appears to be no edition of his works after 1515. Mayer's assertion, incidentally, that there were only two editions of Chariteo's poetry in the first half of the sixteenth century is, however, incorrect.[50] In addition to those of 1509 and 1515, there is a Naples edition of 1506 and Vaganay lists a Venice edition of 1507. It is clear at least that both the vast reputation of Serafino and the comparatively minor successes of Chariteo are closely linked chronologically to the periods in which they were actually producing their works, and the same is true in the case of Tebaldeo. The latter poet lived on until 1537, but in his later years he more or less abandoned vernacular poetry, and one finds his work best represented in publications between 1498 and 1508. Though there is an edition as late as 1550, the number of editions of his works at no time approaches the concentration that one finds in these few years around the turn of the century. As one would expect, the popular poets of the early sixteenth century are gradually overtaken in later years by younger men. Thus a writer such as Olimpo da Sassoferrato (*c.* 1486 – *c.* 1540), who is usually considered to be a very minor figure in the development of early French Petrarchism, was enjoying considerable success in Italy from about 1518 onwards. In the period 1520–50 it is difficult to find two successive years in which no work of his appeared, and in terms of publications he is far ahead of Serafino. Following his death, he too suffered a decline in popularity. I have traced thirty-six editions of his work, only four of them published later than 1550, and I can find no evidence for Mayer's claim that 'Olimpo ne devint vraiment célèbre que dans la deuxième moitié du siècle'.[51]

Of course, if Scève was really interested in poets like Serafino, it is quite possible that he was following Italian fashions at a distance, rather than being intimately acquainted with them. Vianey saw no problem in postulating a time lag between developments in Italy and those in France: he considered that the influence of Serafino in France reached its peak with the publication of the *Délie* in 1544, that the Bembist movement in Italy reached its climax in 1545, and that Bembist influence in France begins with the publication of the *Olive* in 1549. Weber is in complete agreement and he maintains that the *Délie* was written under the influence of 'la préciosité raffinée de Tebaldeo et de Serafino', which gave way, in the years 1549–55, to the 'pétrarquisme élégant et plus classique de Bembo et de ses disciples'.[52] What convinces me finally, however, of the relative unimportance of the Italian contribution to the *Délie* is the nature of the borrowings from Italian which the collection contains. These borrowings are frequently trivial and generally belong to thematic areas in which the French and Italian traditions were already close together. The available evidence suggests, I think, that 'Italianism' penetrated the Lyon cultural milieu very gradually and often in an indirect way, in the form of proverbs, clichés, and the repetition of odd lines of poetry here and there. Nothing in the *Délie* suggests anything as dramatic as an invasion.

We may pass on to consider the nature of some of the probable borrowings from Italian which the *Délie* contains. The case of dizain 100 is entirely typical of the way in which Scève sometimes renders, after the manner of an Italian poet, a theme which had long been current in the French tradition. The poem ends with the line:

Vers toy suis vif, & vers moy je suis mort.

Serafino has the line:

> Che in me morte son io, è in te son vivo.[53]

Has Scève borrowed the line directly from Serafino? I really do not see how one could be sure one way or the other, and I am certain that the matter is of no importance. Saulnier notes the banality of the theme, concluding 'il est probable néanmoins que le vers de Serafino ... a chanté dans sa mémoire [i.e. Scève's], plus ou moins détaché sur un arrière-plan confus', and this seems as reasonable a supposition as any.[54] We may note that Serafino's line comes from the middle of a *Capitolo* (No. xvii) some seventy lines in length, and while it is quite plausible to suppose that Scève remembered the line directly, it is just as likely that the borrowing, if it is one, came to him in some indirect way. The apparent reference to Serafino in dizain 206 is similarly vague, trivial, and confined to a single phrase:

> Dueil traistre occulte, adoncques tu m'assaulx,
> Comme victoire a sa fin poursuyvie,
> Me distillant par l'Alembic des maulx
> L'alaine, ensemble & le poulx de ma vie.[55]

> Poi morte sciogli, è leghi la chatena
> In un momento, faccia di me stratio,
> La voce perdi, i polsi con la lena.[56]

While the same could be said of the parallel between Scève and Serafino in dizain 132:

> Le bon Nocher se monstre en la tempeste,
> Et le Souldart au seul conflict se prœuve ...

> Comporta il marinar fortuna è vento
> Sol per venire al desiato porto;
> Il bon soldato mai cura di stento,
> Perché aspetta la preda per conforto ... [57]

Both passages refer to the soldier and the sailor, but the similarities are otherwise extremely vague. In the same way one can see a possible parallel between some lines of Serafino and the opening of dizain 98, but I do not think the resemblances are very significant:

> Quando dagli alti monti scende l'ombra
> E discaccian le stelle il chiaro giorno,

Ogni stanco animal se posa à l'ombra,
E se discorda il faticar del giorno.
Ahi lasso! io stento è piango . . .[58]

Le Dieu Imberbe au giron de Thetys
Nous fait des montz les grandz umbres descendre:
Moutons cornuz, Vaches, & Veaulx petitz,
En leurs parcz clos serrez se viennent rendre.

This kind of poetry is to be found anywhere. Compare the following lines by Marot, for example:

Aussi le soir, que les trouppeaulx espars
Estoient serrez & remis en leurs parcs . . .[59]

These lines provide a much closer parallel linguistically to ll. 3–4 of Scève's poem, but I see no reason to suppose that there is a direct connection here, any more than I think there is necessarily one between Scève and Serafino. In general it would be fair to say that Scève's alleged borrowings from Serafino are never of the kind one would wish to linger over, for they never have much effect on the quality of the poetry in the *Délie*. As a final example I shall compare dizain 355 with the opening of a strambotto by Serafino, not because the connections here are any more apparent than in the other extracts I have given but because each of the two poems is, in its own way, typical of its author's work in certain respects. We have the measured and complex lines of Scève, with the emergence of an arresting image in the final line; and we have Serafino in virtuoso mood, witty and extravagant:

L'Aulbe venant pour nous rendre apparent
Ce, que l'obscur des tenebres nous cele,
Le feu de nuict en mon corps transparent,
Rentre en mon cœur couvrant mainte estincelle,
    Et quand Vesper sur terre universelle
Estendre vient son voile tenebreux,
Ma flamme sort de son creux funebreux,
Ou est l'abysme a mon cler jour nuisant,
Et derechef reluit le soir umbreux,
Accompaignant le Vermisseau luisant.[60]

Invisibil ne vo per piaggie è campi,
Ché 'l fumo del mio ardor mi tien nascosto,
Et se talhor del pecto escono i vampi,
Mi fan parer qual lucciola d'agosto . . .[61]

There could be no better example of the distance which so
frequently separates the poetry of Scève from that of Serafino
on every level. Scève's dizain is constructed as a single
movement and a parallel between the natural phenomena and
the poet's emotions underlines this movement in a way that is
characteristic of a number of Scève's finer poems. With the
coming of dawn the poet's nightly torment of passion
withdraws into his heart, that it to say his passion, fearing
detection under the growing brightness of day, becomes less
physical and more spiritual. When the evening star appears,
however, his passion reasserts itself and this is symbolized by the
appearance of the glow-worm. The symbol is ideal, for the
glow-worm's rather mysterious arrival every night exactly
parallels the emotional description of the poet's nocturnal state:
'Le feu de nuict en mon corps transparent . . .'. I doubt whether
Scève was led to this by the memory of Serafino flitting about
the countryside like a firefly, but I suppose any judgement in
this matter must be a subjective one.

What we have said of the parallels between Scève and
Serafino applies equally to most of the similarities and affinities
which critics have seen between Italian poets and the *Délie*.
Look, for example, at the two possible borrowings from
Chariteo which McFarlane mentions in his edition of the *Délie*.
We have Chariteo's

> Di lei, per cui, morendo, al mondo vissi,[62]

to set beside the opening of dizain 7:

> Celle beaulté, qui embellit le Monde
> Quand nasquit celle en qui mourant je vis . . .

and similarly we have the line from dizain 274

> Je cours soubdain, ou mes tourmentz m'appellent

to set beside Chariteo's

> Dove 'l dolor mi chiama io vo correndo.[63]

McFarlane suggests three parallels between Scève and Sannazaro
(1456–1530), of which one is interesting by virtue of the fact
that it demonstrates Scève's acquaintance with a specific Italian
poem: both the opening and closing lines of dizain 48 are
translated from the same Sannazaro sonnet. These lines contain

nothing, however, which could not equally well have derived from the native French tradition:

> Si onc la Mort fut tresdoulcment chere,
> A l'Ame doulce ores cherement plaict . . .
>   Dont, comme au feu le Phœnix, emplumée
> Meurt, & renaist en moy cent fois le jour.[64]

As far as the poet Britonio is concerned, McFarlane suggests a parallel between his 'Tra la speranza disperar mi fate' and Scève's 'Mon esperance est a non esperer' in dizain 70; but readers of Marot's rondeau beginning 'En esperant, espoir me desespere' will recognise that Scève's line hardly requires comment in this context. One could go on to look at dizain 102, which contains a vague parallel with a passage from the Italian prose writer Leone Ebreo; one could look at dizain 135, which is a partial translation of a sonnet by Vittoria Colonna; or at dizain 11, which may owe something to Poliziano. But the total effect of all these parallels is not a very powerful one. Instances where Scève's borrowings from Italian obviously add something memorable to his poetry are extremely rare. I would mention in this connection the single obvious borrowing from Bembo's *Rime* in the *Délie*, the zeugma in dizain 423:

> Vois mesurant & les champs, & mes peines.

> vo misurando i campi e le mie pene . . .[65]

I would mention also the first line of dizain 31 of the *Délie*, one of the finest lines of the whole collection, which is in fact a more or less direct translation from the Italian poet Martelli:

> Les tristes Sœurs plaingnoient l'antique offense . . .

> Piangendo il Rosignuol l'antiche offese . . .[66]

The reference here is to the legend of Tereus and the two sisters Procne and Philomela which one finds in the Greek writers Apollodorus and Pausanias, and in the sixth book of Ovid's *Metamorphoses*. The action of the legend springs from the rape of Philomela by her brother-in-law Tereus and the eventual transformation of the two sisters into a nightingale and a swallow. I cannot suggest why Scève should have chosen to remove the reference to the nightingale in his version of Martelli's line. The two birds are not specifically named in

Ovid's account either, but I doubt whether that is at all relevant. A third example of a beneficial use of an Italian source in the *Délie* concerns dizain 342. As Weber points out,[67] Scève does not usually take over any picturesque details from the Italians, but here is an exception; the poem ends with the lines:

> Ainsi Amour aux larmes de ses yeulx
> Ses aeles baigne, a gré se reposant.

The preceding lines tell how Délie bursts into tears whenever the poet criticises her and Scève then evokes a picture of a nightingale bathing its feathers in a spring shower; he is then able to bring together these two seemingly unrelated incidents in the final couplet of the poem, in a way that derives almost certainly from the following lines of Ariosto's *Orlando furioso*:

> Era il bel viso suo, quale esser suole
> da primavera alcuna volta il cielo,
> quando la pioggia cade, e a un tempo il sole
> si sgombra intorno il nubiloso velo.
> E come il rosignuol dolci carole
> mena nei rami alor del verde stelo,
> così alle belle lagrime le piume
> si bagna Amore, e gode al chiaro lume.[68]

In the event I find Ariosto's lines superior to Scève's, but then I have indicated that I do not think Scève is in general much interested in evocative descriptions of natural scenes.

Was Scève intimately acquainted with the work of Bembo, Martelli, and Ariosto? There is no means of knowing. He does not make an obvious use of Bembo or Ariosto anywhere else in the *Délie*, and only one other dizain (No. 27) shows any affinity with Martelli's poetry. It is true that some members of the Martelli family were resident in Lyon and this may have some significance.[69] Lodovico Martelli, the poet, was scarcely a major figure in Italian literature, and there seem to have been only three editions of his poetry by the time the *Délie* was published. In general I think it probable that Scève's very sparing use of his Italian 'sources' indicates that he did not have a particularly wide-ranging knowledge of Italian literature, though I do not see how one could ever be certain either way. Of course some critics have suggested that the really important influence on Scève is not the poetry of contemporary or near-contemporary

Italians but the work of Petrarch himself. D. G. Coleman and
D. Fenoaltea are two proponents of this view and I should like
to examine the available evidence now.[70] Certainly one can
draw a number of linguistic parallels between Scève and
Petrarch, though once again it is often very difficult to be
certain that they derive from direct acquaintance. Thus there
may be some relationship between the lines from dizain 26:

> près de ton œil
> Je me congele: ou loing d'ardeur je fume

and Petrarch's 'arder da lunge ed agghiacciar da presso', but
such examples are notoriously problematic, as we have seen.[71]
Perhaps a sixteenth-century reader would have immediately
recognised the reference to Petrarch and experienced that kind
of intellectual *frisson* that a twentieth-century reader expects
from encountering Dante in T. S. Eliot or Homer in Ezra
Pound. But if Scève is really alluding to Petrarch consciously in
this way one cannot help but wonder whether the effort was
worthwhile, for the results seem to be of minimal benefit to the
poetry. McFarlane suggests (p. 367) that 'it is not without
significance that a Petrarchan echo should be found in the first
and the last lines [of the *Délie*]', and that Scève's collection opens
and closes 'with a discreet homage to Petrarch' (p. 481). If that
is so, then the homage is indeed discreet, for the Petrarchan echo
in dizain 1 escaped Parturier altogether:

> L'Oeil trop ardent en mes jeunes erreurs
> Girouettoit, mal cault, a l'impourveue . . .

McFarlane sees here a parallel with the opening sonnet of the
Canzoniere:

> Voi ch'ascoltate in rime sparse il suono
> di quei sospiri ond' io nudriva 'l core
> in sul mio primo giovenile errore
> quand' era in parte altr' uom da quel ch' i' sono . . .[72]

Perhaps Scève's phrase 'en mes jeunes erreurs' did suggest 'in sul
mio primo giovenile errore' and thus the whole world of the
Canzoniere to a cultured sixteenth-century reader. Perhaps Scève
had so thorough a knowledge of Petrarch that isolated lines and
phrases came to him quite naturally in the course of composing
a particular dizain. On the other hand, it is equally possible that
these occasional lines are the indirect echoes of the vast corpus of

Italian literature whose reputation is recognised, but whose content has been only superficially absorbed. As D. G. Coleman points out, the phrase 'giovenile errore' is also to be found in Serafino and in Bembo,[73] and I would be dubious about attributing Scève's 'jeunes erreurs' to any specific source.

The final dizain of the *Délie*, however, may well contain a conscious allusion to Petrarch, though to the *Trionfi* rather than the *Canzoniere*:

> Nostre Genevre ainsi doncques vivra
> Non offensé d'aulcun mortel Letharge.

> forse che 'ndarno mie parole spargo,
> ma io v' annunzio che voi sete offesi
> da un grave e mortifero letargo.[74]

The Italian lines are from the *Trionfo del tempo*, and if Scève is really alluding to them in his final dizain, the point would be a very subtle one. For Petrarch time is a force which will overcome everything, whereas for Scève the evergreen juniper tree ('Nostre Genevre') is a symbol of everlasting love. Scève does refer to Petrarch specifically on occasion, though he never seems to be saying more than almost everyone must have known. In dizain 388 there is the inevitable reference to the Laura/laurel pun so common in Petrarch:

> Donc ce Thuscan pour vaine utilité
> Trouve le goust de son Laurier amer:
> Car de jeunesse il aprint a l'aymer . . .

The rather fine dizain 417 makes reference to Petrarch's stay in Avignon, but he is once again the conventional Tuscan Apollo who spent his youth in love:

> Fleuve rongeant pour t'attiltrer le nom
> De la roideur en ton cours dangereuse . . .
> Baingnant les piedz de celle terre heureuse
> Ou ce Thuscan Apollo sa jeunesse
> Si bien forma, qu'a jamais sa vieillesse
> Verdoyera a toute eternité . . .

Elsewhere in the *Délie* one finds a number of possible parallels between Scève and Petrarch, though the total is really very small. The opening of Petrarch's sonnet 'La gola e 'l sonno e l'oziose piume' has some affinity with the opening of dizain 100 of the *Délie*, 'L'oysiveté des delicates plumes', and l. 11 of the same Petrarch sonnet provides the final line of dizain 414:

dice la turba al vil guadagno intesa
Et du sot Peuple au vil gaing intentif.

But most of the parallels that have been drawn between Scève and Petrarch are of the most superficial kind: Scève, for example, uses the phrase 'Suave odeur' in dizain 10, while Petrarch has 'soavi odor' in the *Triumphus Cupidinis*. And there are numerous cases where it is impossible to decide whether Scève is following Petrarch directly or simply drawing on the common stock of images and devices that are common to both the French and the Italian traditions.

Critics such as D. G. Coleman and D. Fenoaltea would, however, wish to go beyond an examination of thematic and linguistic parallels and they see thc *Délie* as Scève's attempt to transpose the essential *spirit* of the *Canzoniere* into the French poetic tradition. Such a view seems to me misguided. Of course Scève can write like Petrarch. He can also write in an extravagant manner like Serafino: consider dizain 360, for example, where the poet likens his sobbing to the firing of a canon. But the fact that he can write in a manner vaguely reminiscent of someone else is hardly very significant. Scève does express a desire for solitude in dizain 262, 'Je vois [= je vais] cherchant les lieux plus solitaires' and Petrarch does express a similar desire in the sonnet beginning 'Cercato ò sempre solitaria vita', but such a comparison does little to illuminate the work of either poet. At the level of vague 'affinities' the comparative method breaks down completely and becomes simply the vehicle for the expression of individual preferences. I include merely one example of this kind of comparison, and leave the reader to make of it what he will. D. Fenoaltea suggests that Petrarch's sonnet 'Per mezz' i boschi inospiti e selvaggi' may have influenced the composition of dizain 262 of the *Délie*:

Je vois cherchant les lieux plus solitaires
De desespoir, & d'horreur habitez,
Pour de mes maulx les rendre secretaires,
Maulx de tout bien, certes, desheritez,
Qui de me nuire, & aultruy usitez,
Font encor paour, mesme a la solitude,

Sentant ma vie en telle inquietude,
Que plus fuyant & de nuict, & de jour
Ses beaulx yeulx sainctz, plus loing de servitude
A mon penser sont icy doulx sejour.[75]

Per mezz'i boschi inospiti e selvaggi
onde vanno a gran rischio uomini et arme,
vo securo io, ché non po spaventarme
altri che 'l Sol ch' à d'Amor vivo i raggi;

e vo cantando, o penser miei non saggi,
lei che 'l ciel non poria lontana farme,
ch' i' l'ò negli occhi, e veder seco parme
donne e donzelle, e sono abeti e faggi.

Parmi d'udirla, udendo i rami e l'òre
e le frondi, e gli augei lagnarsi, e l'acque
mormorando fuggir per l'erba verde.

Raro un silenzio, un solitario orrore
d'ombrosa selva mai tanto mi piacque;
se non che dal mio Sol troppo si perde.[76]

The Petrarch sonnet is beautifully done and it has an extraordinarily pathetic quality. It is entirely straightforward in its approach and in the play on such commonplaces as Sun = Laura there is no intellectual or abstract preoccupation. The aim is to communicate a particular feeling through the elements of the natural world which surround the poet, not to explore the complex inner workings of the emotions, and in many of Petrarch's finest poems we find a similar attitude. Santayana is quite right when he says that Petrarch's art is greater than his thought: 'In the quality of his mind there is nothing truly distinguished. The discipline of his long and hopeless love brings him little wisdom, little consolation. He is lachrymose and sentimental at the end, as at the beginning, and his best dream of heaven, expressed, it is true, in entrancing verse, is only to hold his lady's hand and hear her voice.'[77] So much of Petrarch's strength lies in the entrancing verse, and it is for this reason that he is so difficult to imitate. In the twentieth century he must be one of the least translated of all the major European poets, and it is easy to see why. Many of Petrarch's finest lines are untranslatable in exactly the same way as many of Racine's, and of course they have to stand entirely alone, without the benefit of drama. You can never really hope to translate the thirty-sixth line of *Phèdre*: 'La fille de Minos et de Pasiphaé'; nor can you do much with Petrarch's 'Una candida cerva sopra l'erba / verde m'apparve ...'. Both fragments display a perfect harmony between the sounds of the words and the conventions of the metre, and this harmony belongs for ever to the poetic tradition from which it derives. The literal translation into free verse which Paul Valéry made of the Petrarch lines shows how little the *meaning* of the Italian contributes to the delightful quality of the poetry. 'Une candide cerve sur l'herbe verte / m'apparut ...' is a long way from the spirit of the original,[78] just as the English line 'The daughter of Minos and Pasiphae' is scarcely able to convey any impression of the strength of Racine's alexandrine.

Petrarch's extraodrinary lyric gifts have not always been received with total enthusiasm, as Santayana's comments indicate. The poet Cornelio Castaldi (1463–1537) was similarly dubious about the benfits of entrancing verse, and he wrote '... mai non mi parrà poeta / chi sol l'orecchio mio pasce col canto'.[79] But as far as Scève is concerned, the important point is to realise that he is almost never concerned with lyrical beauty as such. At his best and at his worst his natural tendency is towards the complex and the abstract, towards argument and exploration, rather than lyrical description and the straightforward communication of sentiment.

Whatever the direct influence of Petrarch may have been on Ronsard and du Bellay, their love poetry from the very beginning is much closer to the spirit of the *Canzoniere* than is the love poetry of the *Délie*. It is sometimes suggested that Scève is a transitional figure between the world of the Rhétoriqueurs and the poetry of the Pléiade, but I can find little to support such a point of view. Schutz, in his work on Parisian private libraries in the sixteenth century, similarly concludes that 'the Pléiade stepped into a virtual vacuum as far as lyric poetry was concerned', and he says 'it seems dangerous to assume ... that the Petrarchist atmosphere pervaded the larger public ... this is one case ... where large segments of the public, even of the intellectual public, did not participate in movements we consider characteristic of the Renaissance until these movements were well under way'.[80] Even with regard to such commonplace devices as the antithesis, there is a marked difference between Scève's technique and that of his Italian predecessors or his French successors. Saulnier notes: 'Il est remarquable que Scève, contrairement aux Pétrarquistes, pratique peu, en somme, l'antithèse comme procédé de développement, animant une tirade.'[81] What one finds far more often in Scève is the use of antithetical word-groups, and Saulnier lists a large number of these: *vie morte, douce servitude, douce cruauté, doux venin, douce bataille, heureux malheur, certaine doubtance*, and so on. Such word-groups belong to the tradition of the *Roman de la Rose* and the poetry of Alain Chartier, rather than to the world of the Petrarchists or the Pléiade, and Dottin makes this clear when he refers to the influence of the *Jardin de plaisance*:

> C'est certainement à cette esthétique [the rhetoric of the *Jardin*] bien plus qu'à celle du pétrarquisme (assez faiblement représentée avant 1540) que l'on doit ce goût pour le style 'par contradictions', où l'antithèse, encore parfois reserrée dans une alliance de mots comme du temps de Chartier ('triste plaisir et douloureuse joie') se trouve le plus souvent répartie entre les deux sections du vers.[82]

I should like to conclude this chapter with a brief discussion of the contribution of the Italian prose-writer Sperone Speroni (1500–88) to the poetry of the *Délie*. Speroni is the only Italian writer that I can be sure Scève has read extensively, and I think he almost certainly came into contact with Speroni's work at a late stage, probably in the last two years before the publication of the *Délie* in 1544. Speroni was a writer of dialogues and one can easily see why Scève should have been attracted to this kind of Italianism, rather than to the poetry of the Petrarchists. The collected *Dialogi di Messer Speron Sperone* appeared in Venice in 1542, though the first of these, concerned with the nature of love and jealousy and entitled *Dialogo d'Amore*, had been written as early as 1528. The dialogues are an important source not only for Scève but for du Bellay also, since the latter lifted a great deal of the material for his *Deffence et illustration de la langue françoyse* directly from Speroni's *Dialogo delle Lingue*. As far as Scève is concerned, one finds a reminiscence of Speroni in almost every dizain of the *Délie* from 426 onwards, and as these dizains were almost certainly composed at a late date, there is no reason to suppose that Scève's acquaintance with Speroni's work goes back any further than the 1542 edition of the dialogues. Scève's borrowings from Speroni are taken, with one exception, from the *Dialogo d'Amore*, and involve the reproduction both of important images and of trivial details. A good example of the way an image is taken over may be found in dizain 141 (the only dizain to contain a reminiscence of Speroni outside the group 426–end): Scève begins his poem in a manner which derives directly from Speroni:

> Comme des raiz du Soleil gracieux
> Se paissent fleurs durant la Primevere,
> Je me recrée aux rayons de ses yeulx . . .

Speroni had written of the way in which the lover forms an image of the beloved within his soul, 'della cui vista si pasca l'Amore che ella governa, non altramente che de razi del sole si pascono e fiori la primavera',[83] and this image leads Scève on to make a comparison of his own with the play on *raiz/rayons*:

> Comme des raiz . . .
> Je me recrée aux rayons de ses yeulx.

In dizain 446, a poem Béguin considers to mark the summit of the whole sequence, the final image is also taken from Speroni:

> Quand sur la nuict le jour vient a mourir,
> Le soir d'icy est Aulbe a l'Antipode.

'Com' hora non è giorno per tutt' il mondo, ma il nostro vespro è meza notte ad altrui, & la sera di questo hemisperio è l'alba dell' altro.'[84] While the image of the sponge in dizain 439 derives from the same source:

> Bien que raison soit nourrice de l'ame,
> Alimenté est le sens du doulx songe
> De vain plaisir, qui en tous lieux m'entame,
> Me penetrant, comme l'eau en l'esponge.

The illusion of pleasure saps the life-blood of the poet, just as a sponge absorbs water. The first half of the comparison is expressed in a traditional combination of abstractions, *sens*, *raison*, and *ame*, while the concrete image is taken from Speroni: 'Vorrebbe adunque lo amante non abbracciare la cosa amata, ma vivo et intero per entro lei penetrare, non altramente che l'acqua passi la spugna . . .'[85] It is interesting to note that Scève in general makes little use of direct comparisons introduced by *comme*, and in dizains 141 and 439 we have two examples where such a technique is employed in connection with the Italian

source material. Further themes which are treated by Scève in
the manner of Speroni are those dealing with Glaucus in dizain
436, Semele in dizain 443, Diotima in dizain 439, and Orpheus
in dizain 445.[86]

Of course the results of Scève's borrowings from Speroni are
not always particularly interesting. The opening of dizain 441,
for example, follows Speroni very closely, but the impression
the lines create is a very conventional one:

> Doncques apres mille travaulx, & mille,
> Rire, plorer, & ardoir, & geler:
> Apres desir, & espoir inutile,
> Estre content, & puis se quereller,
> Pleurs, plainctz, sanglotz, souspirs entremesler,
> Je n'auray eu, que mort, & vitupere!

It has been pointed out that Scève makes little use of the
extended antithesis and technically this example is thus worth
noting. Worth noting from a different point of view is Scève's
use of Speroni in dizain 443, for this demonstrates the dangers of
trying to reproduce too exactly the source material at one's
disposal:

> Combien qu'a nous soit cause le Soleil
> Que toute chose est tresclerement veue:
> Ce neantmoins pour trop arrester l'œil
> En sa splendeur lon pert soubdain la veue.

'cosi, come tutto ch'el Sole con la sua luce sia cagione ch' egli si
veda ogni cosa, nondimeno per troppo affissarsi nel suo
splendore, perde l'occhio la vista.'[87] The two Italian forms *si
veda* and *la vista* become a single form *veue* in French, and the
demands of poetry inevitably place the same word rather
awkwardly at the rhyme in ll. 2 and 4, while in the final lines of
the dizain one can see how a strict adherence to the Italian text
produces a very convoluted syntax:

> Comme si lors en moy tout estonné
> Semeles fust en presence ravie
> De son Amant de fouldre environné,
> Qui luy ostast par ses esclairs la vie.

The corresponding lines in Speroni are: 'non altramente che
Semele alla presentia di Giove suo amante, di baleni, & di
folgori circondato, perdesse la vita.' Scève preserves the phrase

'di baleni, & di folgori circondato' in 'de fouldre environné',
but the phrase 'alla presentia di Giove suo amante' is split rather
illogically around the rhyme 'en presence ravie / De son
Amant'. This enjambement also produces an awkward
repetition in the ninth line, 'De son Amant de fouldre
environné', while the phrase 'par ses esclairs' in l. 10 is an
addition which explains but adds nothing to the poetry. It is
interesting to see that some of the borrowings from Speroni
indicate how close the French and Italian traditions were in
certain areas. The gnomic statement at the end of dizain 430
would not lead one to suspect an Italian model, or indeed any
model at all:

> Et vrayement n'est point aymant celluy,
> Qui du desir vit hors de l'esperance.

And the same could be said of the ending of dizain 426:

> Mais seurement celluy ne peult trouver
> En aultruy paix, qui a soy donne guerre

or of the ending of dizain 427:

> Aussi comment serois je a elle uny,
> Qui suis en moy oultrément divisé?

All three passages are, however, literal translations of passages
from Speroni.

Of course it is possible to argue that all these obvious
borrowings may simply depend on the fact that Scève was
reading Speroni very close in time to the period in which the
final dizains of the *Délie* were being composed. The parallels
between Scève and the Italian Petrarchist poets may be less
obvious and less numerous because he had had time to absorb
what they had to offer. However, I believe that Scève's interest
in Speroni is a credible meeting of similar minds and
temperaments, whereas he has few natural affinities with either
the Petrarchist poets or with Petrarch himself. There are bound
to be possible parallels between Scève and the Italian poets
wherever one looks, but that is in the nature of love poetry,
where the content and the means of expression are bound to
remain vaguely similar. I have tried to show that the
Petrarchism of the *Délie* is a largely superficial affair, though no
doubt Scève, if he was an ambitious man, would have

encouraged any Italianate interpretations of his sequence as that would have fitted clearly into a developing fashion. Scève at his best and at his worst seems to me far from exhibiting any profound Italian sympathies, and if there is much in his work which is now capable of attracting us I do not think he ever had a conscious desire to revolutionise the development of French love poetry. For that we must await the Pléiade. As Marcel Françon put it, 'ce qu'il y a de nouveau parmi ces poètes de la Pléiade, c'est la volonté déclarée de s'insurger contre le passé', whereas the earlier French poets such as Jean Lemaire de Belges and Clément Marot 'se contentaient d'introduire dans leurs poésies des thèmes et des genres nouveaux qui se juxtaposaient naturellement à ceux qu'ils avaient hérités de leurs prédécesseurs français'.[88] Though Scève was in many ways a more original poet than Jean Lemaire or Marot, he belongs quite clearly with them and his place in a long tradition of French love poetry is quite secure.

4 Love and the problems of abstraction

I have at various times in the course of this book raised the question of abstraction, and I have suggested that one of the principal contributions which Ronsard and du Bellay made to the development of French love poetry was to free it from the abstract tendencies which had dominated so much of the poetry of their predecessors. Of course as soon as one begins to look more closely at the subject the lines become blurred, but I think there is a basic change between the *Délie* and the *Olive*, and this is to a large extent due to a conscious attempt on du Bellay's part to externalise the emotional content of his poetry, to relate emotional events or descriptions of the beloved to concrete aspects of the visible world, rather than to the abstract world in which Scève seems so very much at home. In the present chapter I would like to say a little more about the nature of this abstract world, so that my remarks on Ronsard and du Bellay in the final chapter may be set in a proper perspective. In fact wherever you look in the *Délie* you cannot but be struck by the intensely dense and abstract nature of much of Scève's poetry, and I think this is the main reason why the *Délie* was so long denied any kind of critical acclaim. There is a fairly obvious strain of linguistic abstraction running through the whole work, and in addition a much more complex form of abstraction which has its roots deep in the courtly tradition, and in medieval techniques of abstract/allegorical presentation. I do not wish to say much about the linguistic abstraction in the *Délie*, for in general it explains itself:

> Je contendrois par dessus la victoire:
> Mais hazardant hazard en mes malheurs,
> Las je me fais despouille a mes douleurs,
> Qui me perdantz, au perdre me demeurent,
> Me demeurantz seulement les couleurs
> De mes plaisirs, qui, me naissantz, me meurent.   [dizain 52]

This delight in verbal game playing is characteristic of certain kinds of poetry in many languages, and it obviously caused

some people a great deal of pleasure. One may compare the
following lines from a poem by the troubadour Marcabru:

> Mos talans e sa semblansa
> So e no so d'un entalh,
> Pueys del talent nays semblans
> E pueys ab son dig l'entalha,
> Quar si l'us trai ab mal vesc
> Lo brico, l'autre l'envesca.[1]

The handling of abstractions here may be considered clever, or
artificial, or unnecessarily complicated, but I doubt whether the
result is what a modern reader would call poetry. The subject-
matter is entirely self-contained and unrelated to anything
outside itself. A very few words are called upon to carry a
complex, if somewhat trivial, argument about the nature of
desire and its outward manifestation, and these words, *talans* and
semblans, are pure abstractions, capable of variation and
extension only on the plane of amorous casuistry. The
abstractions are a fundamental part of the form of the poem, as
can be seen from the rhyme-scheme, and they are closely
involved with the compression of sense that is a characteristic
feature of the poem as a whole, and indeed of a great many
troubadour poems belonging to the tradition of the 'trobar
clus', or 'closed style'.

Whether you like this sort of thing or not is simply a matter
of taste, but one cannot deal with the more general medieval
abstract/allegorical inheritance quite so easily. From the point
of view of the modern reader there is perhaps nothing in the
whole field of medieval love poetry which is so difficult to
accept as the reliance on abstraction to convey sentiment. A
simple comparison will highlight the main problems. Consider
the following short poem:

> The moon has set
> And the Pleiades; it is midnight.
> The hours go by
> And I sleep alone.

You could not date this poem on stylistic grounds. It is in fact
by Sappho and thus probably some two thousand six hundred
years old, but it seems infinitely more modern than much of the
verse in the *Délie*. It has directness and simplicity, and at the
same time a degree of conscious understatement which leaves

almost everything to the reader's imagination. The scene depicted is entirely natural, and any reader could easily envisage himself in a similar situation. But look at the following lines from the *Délie*:

Mes tant longz jours, & languissantes nuictz,
Ne me sont fors une peine eternelle:
L'Esprit estainct de cures, & ennuyz,
Se renovelle en ma guerre immortelle.

The emotions underlying this poem (dizain 245) may well be very similar to those which inspired Sappho's lines, but the effect is quite different. Whatever tendencies towards simplicity and directness one may detect in the first two lines are completely forgotten when one reads ll. 3–4. There, as so often, Scève brings in an abstract figure to explain what is going on, and this invariably seems to distance the emotional content of the verse. It is almost as if the poet cannot conceive of feeling anything himself and has to record all his experiences through an intermediary. Where an abstraction is personalised to some extent, where the presentation is to some degree 'allegorical', the problems for the modern reader are admittedly much less serious, but Scève rarely personalises his abstractions, almost never shows any interest in sustained allegory. What he frequently does is to use the debris of the allegorical tradition in a manner for which it is not really suited: that is to say, he frequently employs figures which are intimately associated with the allegorical tradition, but his treatment of those figures tends to be so abstract that they come to serve as little more than a convenient emotional shorthand.

The elevation of the allegorical figure to form part of a coherent system for the communication of sentiment found its most famous expression in the *Roman de la Rose*. Kenneth Clark suggests that no one reads the work any longer, except in universities, and I am sure he is right, but it was one of the most widely read books in Europe for at least three hundred years. It was composed in two very unequal parts by two separate authors between about 1240 and 1280, and was the only medieval work to escape condemnation in du Bellay's *Deffence*:

De tous les anciens poëtes Francoys, quasi un seul, Guillaume du Lauris & Jan de Meun [the two authors of the *Roman de la Rose*], sont dignes d'estre leuz, non tant pour ce qu'il y ait en eux

beaucoup de choses qui se doyvent immiter des modernes, comme
pour y voir quasi comme une premiere imaige de la Langue
Francoyse, venerable pour son antiquité.   [bk. ii, ii]

More than three hundred manuscripts of the *Roman de la Rose*
have survived down to our own time, and there were a large
number of printed editions published between 1481 and 1538.
But it is significant, I think, that after 1538 we have to wait
almost two hundred years before the appearance of another
edition. Du Bellay cannot really avoid paying due compliment
to the *Roman de la Rose* as the most important book of the French
Middle Ages, but the allegorical world of the Romance has no
future in Renaissance France. Personification allegory generally
works best in long narrative works, though we have seen that
there are exceptions to this rule, as in the case of Charles
d'Orléans. Sixteenth-century French love literature is
dominated by the short lyric forms, and no one ever recaptured
the sense of the allegorical family which is so strongly felt all
through Charles's ballades and rondeaux.

Allegory at its best provides an escape into a delightfully
intimate world, peopled by the most complex assortment of
figures, *Amor*, *Avarice*, *Biaus Semblanz*, *Biauté*, *Cortoisie*, *Dangier*,
Honte, *Male Bouche*, *Pitié*, *Raison*, and so on, figures which may
be understood and appreciated on a wide variety of levels.
These figures may exert the simple and profoundly satisfying
attraction which draws us to the personified animals of
children's stories; or they may serve as a convenient means of
coming to terms with complex emotions by separating those
emotions into their constituent parts and analysing the total
effect of their combined contributions. A successful allegory
will always provide the average reader with something in both
these key areas, but the element of personification is of major
importance. The allegory can never really succeed unless you
are convinced, even if only temporarily, that the abstract figures
who appear before you are capable of acting in the manner of
real human beings. An enormous number of figures appear in
the *Roman de la Rose*, and C. Muscatine lists the major ones in an
interesting article published in 1953, entitled 'The emergence of
psychological allegory in Old French Romance'.[2] Some
indication of the popularity which personalised figures enjoyed
throughout the Middle Ages is provided by a further list in J. C.

Laidlaw's edition of the poetical works of Alain Chartier. Laidlaw lists over 120 such figures in the poetry of Chartier and they include all but five of those which had appeared in Muscatine's earlier inventory. Almost two hundred years separate Chartier from the *Roman de la Rose*, but the delight in personified figures remains quite unchanged.

We may now proceed to examine the debris of the allegorical tradition as it emerges from the *Délie*. Dizain 337 provides a useful starting point:

> Veu que Fortune aux accidentz commande,
> Amour au Cœur, & la Mort sur le Corps:
> Occasion conteste a la demande,
> Qu'affection pretent en ses accordz.
> Toy seule, ô Parque, appaises leur discordz,
> Restituant la liberté ravie.
>   Vien donc, heureuse, & desirée envie,
> Nous delyvrant de tant facheux encombres:
> Vien sans doubter, que l'esprit, & la vie
> Par toy fuyront indignez soubz les umbres.

Weber comments on this poem as follows: 'l'expression est si sèche et si dépouillée que la personnification ne se développe même pas en image et rappelle les plus abstraites moralités du XVème siècle.'[3] Indeed there is little to be said in favour of these lines, and even the conclusion of the dizain with its echoes of the closing words of the *Aeneid* fails to move. In fact the whole poem is indicative of the problems which undeveloped allegory or unpersonalised abstractions present to the modern reader. There are seven abstractions in the first four lines, *Fortune*, *Amour, Cœur, Mort, Corps, Occasion, affection*. Some of them clearly derive directly from the allegorical tradition, but there is nothing here which could be called personification allegory. Let it be said at once that the presence or absence of capital letters in the printing of sixteenth-century books is usually of little significance in this context. As Henri Chamard noted in his edition of du Bellay's *Deffence*, Renaissance printers were quite happy to capitalise almost anything, and it would be a certain error to make distinctions concerning the allegorical quality of particular words according to whether their initial letters are capitalised or not. As Saulnier points out, 'la vraie mesure de la qualité "allégorique", c'est la précision du mouvement humain dont se trouve dotée une notion',[4] and on this basis we cannot

reasonably talk of allegory in connection with dizain 337 of the
Délie. The figures such as *Fortune* in l. 1 are admittedly subjects
of main verbs which are usually associated with the actions of
human beings, but there is much more to allegory than that.
Empson writes: 'Part of the function of an allegory is to make
you feel that two levels of being correspond to one another in
detail, and indeed that there is some underlying reality,
something in the nature of things, which makes this happen.'5

Scève's 'allegorical' figures have left the world of allegory
and have become almost total abstractions, unrelated to
anything except themselves and deprived of the personal
reference which alone can ensure the successsful communication
of emotion. A glance at the *Roman de la Rose* will show the
distance which separates allegory from abstraction. Look, for
example, at the treatment of a figure such as *Fortune* or *Mort*. In
the *Roman de la Rose* we find a powerfully dramatic description
of Fortune's Isle beginning at line 5921, and *Raison* then
proceeds to dramatise the well-known ambiguities in Fortune's
character. Sometimes she appears like a queen, in the most
exquisite apparel, and receives all the honours of the world. But
then we see her with her wheel spinning, wandering through
her abode until she comes to the part that is filthy and decaying,
and there she throws herself to the ground, strips herself naked,
and, realising that she is utterly worthless, she disappears into a
brothel. *Mort* too is graphically described; in the passage
beginning at line 15943 we see her, with her face dyed black,
merciless in her pursuit of every living thing:

> Ainsinc Mort; qui ja n'iert saoule,
> Gloutement les pieces engoule;
> Tant les suit par mer e par terre
> Qu'en la fin toutes les enterre.   [ll. 15965–8]

But *Fortune* and *Mort* in dizain 337 of the *Délie* are simply words,
the latter even being accompanied by the definite article.
Whereas the whole substance of the *Roman de la Rose* depends on
the relationships between its allegorical figures, in the poetry of
Scève those figures survive in an essentially functional capacity,
useful for the manipulation of an argument within the confined
space of the dizain.

Saulnier, like most critics, sees the allegorical tradition as an
essentially static one, and finds no difficulty in bridging the gap

which separates the *Délie* from the *Roman de la Rose*. On the subject of Scève's recurring use of figures like *Fortune*, *Mort*, *Amour*, *Malheur*, *Espoir*, and so on, he writes, 'Les figures allégoriques deviennent les "personnages reparaissants" de Balzac. On n'a plus, dès lors, à tout dire de chaque allégorie, quand on la rencontre une fois: elle se précisera elle-même en chemin, par ses diverses réactions en ses différents engagements.'[6] Such an approach may well be appropriate in the case of earlier 'allegorical' works, but it is scarcely relevant to the *Délie*, for I think none of Scève's figures ever emerges as a positive and unifying character. Of course I cannot hope to judge what a sixteenth-century reader may have thought. It is possible to argue that the accumulated weight of the allegorical tradition made it unnecessary for a poet such as Scève to insist on a human reference for his abstract figures. Perhaps a contemporary reader, faced with dizain 337, would have immediately filled in the allegorical background for himself. I do not think this is a convincing justification for Scève's practice, however, and the way Ronsard and du Bellay almost totally dispensed with the use of juxtaposed abstract figures highlights the considerable problems which the technique entails.

Scève never fully developed any other method of communicating and analysing emotion. He is a writer who produced a number of very fine poems and a considerable number of very fine lines, but his natural instincts always draw him to his abstract figures, and with them he seems entirely at home. Dizain 56 provides further illustration of the point:

Le Corps travaille a forces enervées,
Se resolvant l'Esprit en autre vie.
Le Sens troublé voit choses controvées
Par la memoire en phantasmes ravie.
Et la Raison estant d'eulx asservie
(Non aultrement de son propre delivre)
Me detenant, sans mourir, & sans vivre,
En toy des quatre à mis leur guerison.
   Doncques a tort ne t'ont voulu poursuyvre
Le Corps, l'Esprit, le Sens, & la Raison.

The general technique of this poem is paralleled in numerous other compositions, both in France and in Italy, and further examples may be seen in dizains 107 and 444 of the *Délie*. The

usual method is to introduce a number of abstract figures in the
course of the natural development of the poem, and then to
conclude with a logical statement indicating that the figures are
in some way related. In dizain 56 the poet seeks to show how
various abstract figures all conspire against him. A debilitating
force, which is clearly that of the beloved, affects *Corps*, *Esprit*,
and *Sens*, and thus finally *Raison*, which, although dependent on
the first three figures, is able to see that the salvation of all
depends on Délie alone. Similarly in dizain 444 Scève
introduces the figures *Nature*, *Amour*, *Vertu*, and *Raison* in the
course of his argument, and is then able to conclude that only in
his beloved are all four elements brought together. Such poems
were an obvious source of delight for poet and audience alike,
but the main interest lies in the manipulation of form, rather
than in the particular nature of the abstract figures employed.
Incidentally one may note how dizain 56 and dizain 337 share
three rhymes in *-vie*: we find *ravie*, *envie*, and the simple *vie* in
the latter poem, while in the former we find *vie*, *ravie*, and
asservie. This kind of rhyming pattern is commonly used by
Scève and by numerous other writers of the time, and one can
see how useful abstract figures can be in filling out a line around
the basic rhyming units. Thus in dizain 337 there is the phrase
'l'esprit, & la vie' at the end of l. 9, while in dizain 56 the same
combination produces the vague and unsatisfactory line, 'Se
resolvant l'Esprit en autre vie'. The point is of some interest and
I shall return to it later.

The functional nature of much of the abstraction in the *Délie*
is readily apparent when one sets it beside some of the rare
examples of true allegory in the collection. Consider the
opening lines of dizain 180, for example:

> Quand pied a pied la Raison je costoye,
> Et pas a pas j'observe ses sentiers,
> Elle me tourne en une mesme voye
> Vers ce, que plus je fuiroys voulentiers.

Raison appears here as an independent force, even though
preceded by the definite article, and the allegorical presentation
is sustained over four lines. You can easily visualise what is
going on even if you do not wish to enter into metaphysical
speculations. In particular, the phrase 'j'observe ses sentiers'
relates the concept of Reason to a very easily grasped physical

presence, and for a brief moment we are almost in the world of
Charles d'Orléans, where Reason appears so frequently as a
member of an intimate allegorical family. Charles can write
with total conviction, 'Raison est et sera des miens' (ballade 29),
and this familiarity is something very rare in Scève. The final six
lines of dizain 180 move away from the allegorical presentation
of the opening, and ll. 5–6, though maintaining a vague sense of
the *sentiers* from l. 2, are already involved in an argument which
becomes ever more abstract as the poem proceeds:

> Mais ses effectz en leur oblique entiers
> Tendent tousjours a celle droicte sente,
> Qui plusieursfoys du jugement s'absente,
> Faignant du miel estre le goust amer: [ll. 5–8]

Reason is still the main character, but all visual contact is lost
through the complex oppositions in these four lines. The
argument has an underlying physical basis, but it is not very
easy to grasp. Reason is leading the poet along a path towards
that which he least desires—the recognition that the sweetness
of love is merely an illusion; and this is, of course, always the
proper role of *Raison*, whose tortuous efforts lead invariably
towards the same 'droicte sente', and who in the end convinces
the poet that he must accept what is contrary to his emotional
nature:

> Puis me contrainct quelque mal, que je sente,
> Et vueille, ou non, a mon contraire aymer.   [ll. 9–10]

Thus, though Reason remains the subject throughout, the
completely allegorical treatment of the opening leads to an
ending whose sense can only really be grasped as an abstraction.
One may compare this approach to that of dizain 179 which
serves as a prelude to the poem we have just discussed and
which introduces the theme of the opposition between Love
and Reason. This theme is, of course, an ancient one, and, as A.
D. Scaglione points out, was as much a feature of Jean de
Meun's contribution to the *Roman de la Rose* as it was of
Guillaume de Lorris's.[7] Scève's treatment of the perennial
opposition is strictly allegorical throughout dizain 179 and,
though there is not the easy familiarity of 'Quand pied a pied la
Raison je costoye', the powers of Love and Reason are
presented as independent characters which can act physically on

the poet and influence his actions in different ways. The opening two lines of the poem put forward the case for *Amour*, the following two lines the case for *Raison*, while ll. 5–8 maintain this simple opposition, *Celluy* referring back to *Amour*, and *ceste* to *Raison*:

> Celluy desjà, m'esloingnant de douleur,
> De toy m'asseure, & ceste me desgoute,
> Qui jour & nuict devant les yeulx me boute
> Le lieu, l'honneur, & la froide saison.

The poet is then able to make his conclusion in a logical way which is very easily grasped:

> Dont pour t'oster, & moy, d'un si grand doubte,
> Fuyant Amour, je suivray la Raison.

A further example of sustained allegory in the *Délie* occurs in dizain 260. There we find a completely traditional picture of the lover tossed on the stormy seas of love, about to reach his desired haven—with all that is thereby implied—and being finally thwarted by the violent winds of fortune:

> Sur fraile boys d'oultrecuydé plaisir
> Nageay en Mer de ma joye aspirée,
> Par un long temps, & asseuré plaisir
> Bien pres du Port de ma paix desirée.
>   Ores fortune envers moy conspirée
> M'à esveillé cest orage oultrageux,
> Dont le fort vent de l'espoir courageux
> Du vouloir d'elle, et du Havre me prive,
> Me contraingnant soubz cest air umbrageux
> Vaguer en gouffre, ou n'y à fons ne ryve.

The allegory here is basically of two kinds. On the one hand one finds the use of traditional personified figures such as *fortune* in order to account for the inevitable vagaries of love. On the other, one finds a number of examples of the formula type of allegory that is so common in the poetry of Charles d'Orléans. This formula type is very rare in the *Délie*, and consists of the application of a concrete physical reference to an abstract sensation, as in 'Mer de ma joye' or 'Port de ma paix'. Examples in the poetry of Charles d'Orléans are legion; one could mention such periphrases as 'L'uys de mon cueur', in rondeau 424, or 'le logis / De mon las cueur', in ballade 26. But a poem

such as dizain 260 is the exception in the *Délie*. Scève has in
general little interest in the traditional techniques of allegorical
presentation, and examples of true allegory are normally
confined to a few lines here and there. Thus in dizain 438 the
poet muses in a rather abstract way about the time he is wasting
in the pursuit of a love which promises nothing; and then, as he
thinks of abandoning his quest altogether, the alternatives facing
him are suddenly introduced in a traditional allegorical pattern
which highlights his dilemma clearly:

> J'eschappe a doubte, espoir, ardeur, attente,
> Pour cheoir es mains de la douleur lattente . . .

One may compare the following lines by Charles d'Orléans:

> Temps et temps m'ont emblé Jennesse,
> Et laissé es mains de Viellesse . . .   [rondeau 420]

The advantage of this kind of presentation is that it is extremely
easy to follow. One does not have to pause and analyse the
numerous abstractions which fill Scève's two lines, for the
argument is carried by the general impression of an opposition
created by the juxtaposition of two simple concrete verbs.
Similarly in dizain 276 we find the abstraction of the earlier part
of the poem clarified by the straightforward presentation of the
ending:

> Ou je pensois trouver joye, & plaisir
> J'ay rencontré & tristesse, & douleur.

While the vigorous opening of dizain 91 is based on the same
technique:

> Osté du col de la doulce plaisance,
> Fu mis es bras d'amere cruauté . . .

Such lines as these could easily have been written by Charles
d'Orléans, but Scève's main interests lie elsewhere. He is far
more often involved with superficially complex combinations
of abstractions that have no allegorical reference, and this is
why the argument of so many of his dizains is so difficult to
follow and the decipherment of the argument so frequently
unrewarding.

I think Scève's attitude to allegory and abstraction is
symptomatic of a general decline in the allegorical tradition,

and many of the problems in the *Délie* are a result of his inability to free himself from the debris of that declining tradition. Look, for example, at dizain 419. Weber, in *La Création poétique* (pp. 193–4), relates the attack on Love's stronghold which forms the basis of this poem to the struggle for the rose in the *Roman de la Rose*, but one can see at a glance how great is the distance which separates the two works and how far the allegorical tradition has degenerated:

> Hault est l'effect de la voulenté libre,
> Et plus haultain le vouloir de franchise,
> Tirantz tous deux d'une mesme equalibre,
> D'une portée a leur si haulte emprise:
> Ou la pensée avec le sens comprise
> Leur sert de guide, & la raison de Scorte,
> Pour expugner la place d'Amour forte:
> Sachant tresbien, que quand desir s'esbat,
> Affection s'escarmouche de sorte,
> Que contre vueil, sens, & raison combat.

This description of an attack and the reference to the forces ranged on either side fails to convey any sense of drama. There is no emotional or erotic power in the lines, nothing to suggest that the abstractions have a physical, concrete role to play in the mind of the poet. The few concrete verbs such as *expugner*, *s'escarmouche*, or *combat* do not function as elements in a generally conceived visual presentation; on the contrary, they serve to highlight the extent to which the visual dimension is lacking. The main argument is carried by a large number of unpersonalised abstractions, and it is clearly with these that Scève is most at home. The poet seeks to dislodge the power of love by the use of his will, in the company of *pensée*, *sens*, and *raison*, and out of instinct and tradition he portrays these figures as participants in an allegorical drama. But he is not really interested in that drama. He is attempting to explain something about an emotional situation and he uses the most natural material which comes to hand. It is interesting in this context to look at the work which P. Zumthor and J. Fox have done on the allegorical tradition as it affects the poetry of Charles d'Orléans. For in that poetry we can already see quite clearly the kind of attitudes which led eventually to the highly abstract poetry of the *Délie*. Zumthor and Fox have seen what Saulnier did not: that there is nothing necessarily fixed about the allegorical tradition. Not only can different poets approach the tradition in different ways, but even within the work of a single poet there can be significant changes of attitude.

Zumthor's approach to the question of allegory in the poetry of Charles d'Orléans is essentially a statistical one. He finds that over the years certain allegorical figures decline in frequency, while others are on the increase. For example, *Dangier* is the second most popular personification in the ballades of Charles d'Orléans, but it slips to fourteenth place in the rondeaux, which are compositions of a later date. *Dangier* is what Zumthor terms a 'legs du *Roman de la Rose*', and thus one might suppose that Charles came gradually to reject those figures which depended too obviously on past traditions. Zumthor summarises his findings thus: 'L'évolution que nous observons chez lui . . . va, de ce que je nommerais une fermeture presque totale vers un essai d'ouverture',[8] and by this he means that the changing fortunes of the various allegorical figures in Charles's poetry indicate that the poet was moving away from the closed world of traditional allegory on the path towards symbolism. Zumthor deduces this movement from the decline of figures such as *Amour*, *Fortune*, *Plaisir*, and *Loyauté*, 'personnifications traditionnelles et (pour *Amour* et *Fortune*) de caractère descriptif plus qu'émotif', and the rise of figures such as *Espoir* and *Pensée*, 'désignant sémantiquement, quelle qu'en soit la nuance, une intériorité'. Fox too concludes, independently, that 'the "paysages introspectifs" of symbolism came to interest him [Charles] more than the "paysages moralisés" of allegory'.[9] The change, if it is a real one, would be important, for it would reveal an attempt on the part of Charles to break down the two-layered structure of the allegorical mode. Successful allegory, as I have suggested, relies on the clearly perceived relationship between the character of the personified figure on the one hand, and the range of emotions for which that figure stands on the other. Between the character and the emotion there is in some sense a barrier; as Empson suggests, 'the effect of allegory is to keep the two levels of being very distinct in your mind, though they interpenetrate one another in so many details'.[10] Allegory is a democratic procedure. It explains how things happen by breaking down emotions into several easily-handled parts, and then it dramatises the results for all to see and understand.

Symbolism is a much less democratic affair, for it does not deal
with the known and accepted: it suggests rather than defines, as
Jung points out in his famous definition: 'An allegory is a
paraphrase of a conscious content, whereas a symbol is the best
possible expression for an unconscious content whose nature can
only be guessed, because it is still unknown.'[11] Of course
Zumthor's statistical approach to the allegorical figures in the
poetry of Charles d'Orléans has a number of potential
limitations. One should always beware of drawing artistic
conclusions from tables of figures. *Espoir* does indeed move from
third place of popularity in the ballades to first place in the
rondeaux, while *Pensée* moves from seventh place to sixth.
Raison, another figure which might suggest 'une intériorité',
moves from eleventh place to seventh. A hostile observer would
naturally point out that some of these movements are not very
large, and that in numerical terms the differences may not reflect
anything very significant. Thus *Espoir*, for example, appears
thirty-six times in the ballades and forty-six times in the
rondeaux; *Pensée*, fifteen times and twenty-one; *Raison*, nine
times and eighteen. It might further be argued that the
comparison is not between identical forms, and that such small
numerical differences may be due simply to the structural
differences between ballades and rondeaux. On this point, it is
true, Zumthor argues that a comparison between the ballades
written before 1440 and those written after that date would
confirm his general thesis. That is one finds a decline in the use
of such figures as *Loyauté*, *Tristesse*, *Mort*, and *Dangier*, and an
increase in the frequency of *Merencolie*, *Soussy*, *Nonchaloir*, and
Raison. This might further lead one to enquire, however, why
Tristesse and *Merencolie* are apparently so different in their
'interior' quality, and indeed any close examination of this kind
will inevitably reveal the limitations of a statistical approach.

Nevertheless, I think it reasonable to suggest that there is a
discernible change in the way Charles employs his allegorical
fugures over the years, even if the evolution is not always
completely in conformity with the statistical data. Moreover, as
I have pointed out, Zumthor's conclusions are supported quite
independently by Fox, who also suggests that there is a radical
difference between the work of Charles as a whole and the
world of the *Roman de la Rose*. One might indeed have expected
to find such a difference, but the attitude of most critics has

always been that the allegorical tradition was a fixed and never-ending affair, and little work has been done on the evolution of that tradition in the three hundred years which separate the *Roman de la Rose* from the *Délie*. Fox suggests that 'a particular feature of Charles's characters, distinguishing them from the stock figures of the *Roman de la Rose* tradition, is that they are never wholly exteriorized'. He maintains that the chief role of the allegorical figures in the *Roman de la Rose* was a physical one: 'Though they may reflect mental processes to some extent, their primary source is not a psychological one.' In the poetry of Charles, on the other hand, Fox maintains that much less emphasis is laid on the physical reality of the figures as completely developed characters: Charles's figures 'remain shadowy, unsubstantial and impressionistic.'[12] Such conclusions are, of course, highly relative, and the abstract figures in the poetry of Charles have a much more obvious personality than they do anywhere in the *Délie*, for example, but the evolutionary drift of the allegorical tradition is certainly in the direction that Fox describes, and the poetry of the *Délie* can be seen as a natural further stage in the evolutionary process. Charles's figures may well be more shadowy than those in the *Roman de la Rose*, but he is still able to treat them as personal friends or enemies, and in this connection one finds a frequent use of direct address and the simple concrete verb:

> L'autr' ier alay mon cueur veoir,
> Pour savoir comment se portoit;
> Si trouvay avec lui Espoir
> Qui doulcement le confortoit . . .   [ballade 37]

or:

> Cueur, trop es plain de folie.
> Cuides tu de t'eslongnier
> Hors de nostre compaignie . . .?   [ballade 81]

Most of the figures in the *Délie*, however, seem to have achieved an almost completely non-physical autonomy, devoid of any human reference. When more basic research has been done, it may be possible to chart the fortunes of the allegorical tradition with greater precision, so that one could show, on the one hand, the gradual decline in the physical role of the allegorical figure, and, on the other, the rise of the autonomous

'interior' abstraction. It is this general evolution which led to
the eventual demise of allegory, for the whole force of the
allegorical tradition lay in its ability to communicate sentiment
through the juxtaposition of two clearly perceived levels of
meaning. With the abandonment of one of those levels you can
no longer really speak of allegory. Scève, it is clear, had a
distinct preference for the basically abstract over the basically
allegorical, and this preference has much to do with the
difficulties that his poetry presents to the modern reader.

Most critics who have worked on the *Délie* have tended to
assume that the various abstractions which appear in the course
of the poetry have a meaning which may be more or less
precisely defined. I do not believe this is generally true,
however, and my remarks on the evolution of the
abstract/allegorical tradition may help to explain why.
Consider dizain 143, for example:

> Le souvenir, ame de ma pensée,
> Me ravit tant en son illusif songe,
> Que, n'en estant la memoyre offensée,
> Je me nourris de si doulce mensonge.
>   Or quand l'ardeur, qui pour elle me ronge,
> Contre l'esprit sommeillant se hazarde,
> Soubdainement qu'il s'en peult donner garde,
> Ou qu'il se sent de ses flammes grevé,
> En mon penser soubdain il te regarde,
> Comme au desert son Serpent eslevé.

The poem is rather successful and D. G. Coleman has provided
an interesting analysis.[13] The first four lines speak of the illusory
nature of the kind of happiness which derives from memory,
and then we see how memory works to produce an invasion of
physical desire which breaks in on the dream world of the
opening. At this point the poet's mind offers an image of Délie
to his spirit, thus providing his spirit with its only means of
coming to terms with the invasion and of resisting its effects,
and he compares the healing action of Délie's presence to the
bronze serpent made by Moses as a cure for the victims of the
plague of poisonous snakes which God, in his anger, had sent
down upon the Israelites. Though the argument is carried by a
number of abstractions which have the characteristic effect of
distancing the emotional appeal, the poem retains the reader's

interest because of the arresting image in the final line and because of the fine musical quality of a number of the preceding lines. The poem is obviously not allegorical in any true sense, though the way in which the underlying relationships between the various abstractions is conceived derives in large part from the world of traditional allegory. Because of the direction in which the allegorical tradition has evolved it is not easy to understand the precise meaning of the individual abstract figures—they have become ever more shadowy and internalised, and so, though the general sense of the dizain is clear enough, any attempt to define the precise quality of the various abstractions soon runs into difficulties. D. G. Coleman, for example, maintains that there is a significance in the fact that Délie appears 'en mon penser' in l. 9, whereas in l. 3 only the poet's 'memoyre' is involved. She sees the poem progressing logically towards 'penser' as the poet's highest faculty, but the major objection to this notion of a measured order of ascent is that the abstractions are too loosely employed to support any very rigorous qualitative distinctions. The identity of the 'highest faculty' varies from dizain to dizain and from critic to critic. Thus in D. G. Coleman's doctoral thesis *Ame* and *sens* appear as the highest faculties,[14] while for H. Vernay *Raison* holds the key, aided by *esprit* and *sens*.[15] One notes that the supposed differences between *penser* and the other elements of dizain 143 are scarcely emphasised by the poet. Indeed *penser* is already closely implicated with *souvenir* and both are involved with *ame*. There is no doubt a vague difference between *souvenir* and *memoyre*, the former being more a passive, the latter more an active force, but to try to go much farther than this seems to me unwise. What, for example, is the precise meaning of 'ame de ma pensée'? This straightforward coupling of two unqualified abstractions obviously refers in some way to the very interior nature of memory, but I doubt if the phrase admits of a more complex analysis than that. I suspect that by the time of the *Délie* poets were readily prepared to use abstractions in a more or less functional way and that precise differences between particular figures could be easily ignored in the face of more pressing considerations, such as the demands of metre and of form.

This tendency towards a functional use of abstractions can be seen in the very first dizain of the *Délie*:

> L' Oeil trop ardent en mes jeunes erreurs
> Girouettoit, mal cault, a l'impourveue:
> Voicy (ô paour d'agreables terreurs)
> Mon Basilisque avec sa poingnant' veue
> Perçant Corps, Cœur, & Raison despourveue,
> Vint penetrer en l'Ame de mon Ame.
>   Grand fut le coup, qui sans tranchante lame
> Fait, que vivant le Corps, l'Esprit desvie,
> Piteuse hostie au conspect de toy, Dame,
> Constituée Idole de ma vie.

One can see here two functional patterns centred on a group of abstractions and an accompanying rhyming unit. The first occurs in l. 5. There the poet expresses the developing force of the power of love which affects in turn *Corps*, *Cœur*, and *Raison*, and these abstractions, along with *despourveue* at the rhyme, constitute virtually the whole substance of the line. One may compare this with a line from dizain 115 where one finds the same order of verb, abstract figures, and rhyming element: 'Surpris le Cœur, & l'Ame a l'impourveue...' The useful rhyming unit *a l'impourveue* or *despourveue* inevitably attracts the simple *veue*, as in l. 4 of dizain 1, or l. 2 of dizain 115: 'Tu m'esblouis premierement la veue...' The other example of a functional pattern in the opening dizain of the *Délie* may be seen in ll. 8–10. *Corps* and *Esprit* provide the basis for the antithesis in the eighth line, and the rhyme word *desvie* once again leads naturally to the use of the simple *vie* in the concluding line. This pattern has already been noted earlier and it is one which is capable of quite considerable variation. We find the noun *vie* used in conjunction with a large number of words such as *ravie*, *envie*, *convie*, *poursuyvie*, *deservy*, *suyvie*, *servie*, *desvie*, *assouvie*, and *asservie*, all words that may naturally attract, or are easily adaptable to, the presence of accompanying abstract figures. Of course it will be argued that many poets have made use of such patterns. Abstractions are always of value if you want to fill out or balance a line of poetry. I choose the following examples at random from the poetry of Chariteo:

> L'alma, la mente mia, gli occhi e 'l pensiero,
> Donna, son in pregion nel vostro petto...

and:

> L'Alma resta languendo di dolcezza,
> Oscuri gli occhi & tormentato il core...[16]

In the case of Scève, however, two important points should be made. In the first place his use of abstract patterns is much more extensive than with the majority of poets. In the second place it is clear that where abstractions constitute the whole substance of a line or a poem, in a way that regularly occurs in the *Délie*, attention is more directly called to the existence of functional patterns than would otherwise be the case. A glance at du Bellay's use of the rhymes *vie* and *ravie* in sonnet 94 of the *Olive* is instructive in the present context:

> Mais ce doulx bruit, dont les divins accens
> Ont occupé la porte de mes sens,
> Retient le cours de mon ame ravie.
>
> Voila comment sur le mestier humain
> Non les trois Sœurs, mais Amour de sa main
> Tist & retist la toile de ma vie.

Du Bellay uses the nouns *sens* and *ame*, just as earlier in the poem he has used *penser* and *vouloir*, but these abstractions are not grouped in the linear way Scève so often favours and they are not called upon to carry the main force of the argument. The reader is far more interested by the imagery in the final lines, where the poet argues that Love, rather than the Fates, is the controlling power in his life. The image may not be a spectacular one, but it is certainly a more important element in the poem than any question of abstractions or functional rhyming patterns, and the latter thus pass largely unnoticed.

The relative absence of concrete images in the *Délie* and Scève's tendency to group his abstractions in linear fashion around a rhyming unit produce a number of rather arid lines. The following four examples centred on *vie* show quite clearly the functional nature of the pattern involved:

> Vien sans doubter, que l'esprit, & la vie
> Par toy fuyront indignez soubz les umbres.   [dizain 337]
>
>   Car par ceulx cy le sang bien maigrement,
> Et par les siens tire & l'ame, & la vie.   [dizain 250]
>
> Ce lyen d'or, raiz de toy mon Soleil,
> Qui par le bras t'asservit Ame, & vie . . .   [dizain 12]
>
>   Car te immolant ce mien cœur pour hommage
> Sacrifia avec l'Ame la vie.   [dizain 3]

I think it is important to recognise the existence of these formal patterns and to resist the temptation to seek a precise definition for the individual abstractions which help to make up those patterns. Thus the very symmetrical character of the above examples would lead me to question Saulnier's general definition of the noun *ame* as it appears in the *Délie*. He writes: 'elle représente tout ce qui, de l'homme, s'élève au-dessus de la pure sensibilité et de l'instinct.'[17] To me the combination of *ame* and *vie* conveys merely a vague sense of totality, in exactly the same way as the English phrase 'body and soul', and the point may be further illustrated by setting the example from dizain 3 in its context:

> Car te immolant ce mien cœur pour hommage
> Sacrifia avec l'Ame la vie.
>   Doncques tu fus, ô liberté ravie,
> Donnée en proye a toute ingratitude:
> Doncques espere avec deceue envie
> Aux bas Enfers trouver beatitude.   [ll. 5–10]

Line 6 is clearly the focal point of these few lines. The poet, overcome with love, gives up both *l'Ame* and *la vie*. The direct result is the loss of liberty and the poet concludes with a paradox centred on thwarted love ('deceue envie') and the ironic prospect of eternal bliss in hell. The rhymes *ravie* and *envie* which serve to develop the consequences of l. 6 are clearly underlined by the logical *Doncques* at the beginning of ll. 7 and 9, and McFarlane notes 'the somewhat rigid articulation of the dizain' which such logical pointers entail. It is easy to see how closely the combination of *Ame* and *vie* is related, through the rhyme pattern, to the general structure of the poem, and I think the combination is used simply to indicate the totality of the poet's defeat in love. Saulnier recognises that the word *Ame* in dizain 3 is used only in the vaguest sense, for he writes: L'âme n'est parfois que le séjour de la vie, l'*anima* latine, le souffle vital.'[18] If one sets the three examples of the combination *ame+vie* from dizains 3, 12, and 250, against the example of *esprit+vie* from dizain 337, it will be evident that the difference between *ame* and *esprit* is not very great. When the poet writes 'Vien sans doubter, que l'esprit, & la vie . . .', instead of 'l'ame, & la vie', I am sure he is more concerned with the demands of metre than with questions of definition.

Indeed Saulnier is willing to admit that *esprit* and *ame* may be employed as synonyms on occasion, and that *esprit* and *pensée*, or *entendement* and *memoire* may be similarly used. This raises an obvious problem. Is it reasonable to draw subtle distinctions between particular abstractions when they occur in some dizains and then to suggest that when they occur in others distinctions hardly exist? The complicated relationships between the various figures which Saulnier seeks to establish do not seem to me very relevant to an understanding of Scève's poetry, and I think that any attempt to define the nature of an abstraction in the *Délie* must take account of the evolution we have observed in the medieval abstract/allegorical tradition. The day of the allegorical family is over and many of Scève's abstractions have little more than a functional role to play in his poetry; they have a vague and fluid quality which is ideal for his purposes and largely eludes analysis.

Misconceptions concerning the functional role of many of the abstractions in sixteenth-century poetry are widespread and the point is further illustrated by Weber's comments on some lines by Guy Le Fèvre de la Boderie (1541–98):

> L'Occident, l'Aquilon, l'Orient, le My Jour,
> Thobias, Job, Judith, Esther de lis florie,
> L'histoire, le Moral, Figure, Allégorie
> Cernent corps, Ame, Esprit et la Pensée au tour.

For Weber *ame* is the platonic 'principe vital', *esprit* the 'véhicule passif de la Connaissance', and *pensée* the 'véhicule actif'.[19] Now we know that Guy Le Fèvre was a highly learned man and a considerable scholar, but there is nothing in these lines to suggest that the abstractions have a precisely definable quality which one could discuss in philosophical terms. *Ame*, *Esprit*, and *Pensée* simply constitute a list to match those in the preceding three lines and together they convey the general sense of a totality in a way that is reminiscent of many of the poems in the *Délie*. Variations on these linear patterns abound throughout Scève's collection:

> Dont froide peur surprenant lentement
> Et Corps, & Cœur, à jà l'Ame conquise.   [dizain 66]

> Mon Basilisque avec sa poingnant' veue
> Perçant Corps, Cœur, & Raison despourveue ...   [dizain 1]

There is little internal evidence to suggest that Scève or other
contemporary poets were seriously interested in differentiating
between the various abstractions they employed, except on the
most general level. Figures could apparently be interchanged at
will, as the following two examples from the *Jardin* illustrate:

> Ma bouche rit et ma pensee pleure,
> Mon oeil s'esjoye et mon cueur mauldit l'heure . . .
>
> Ma bouche rit et mon cueur pleure . . .[20]

Pensée and *cœur* are evidently synonymous here, the former
being used for the ten-syllable line, the latter for the line of eight
syllables, and in the numerous abstract combinations in the
Délie similar metrical considerations are of obvious importance.
The individual abstract figures may be considered as convenient blocks, easily movable within the line and adaptable to
suit questions of metre, variety, or simply the poet's fantasy.
If one compares the examples I quoted earlier of Scève's use
of the combinations *ame+vie* and *esprit+vie* with the following
examples of *ame+sens* and *ame+cœur*, I think it will be agreed
that differences between the abstract figures are slight indeed:

> Qui par sa haulte, & divine excellence   [dizain 6]
> M'estonna l'Ame, & le sens tellement . . .
>
> Le sens, & l'ame y furent tant ravis,
> Que par l'Oeil fault, que le cœur la desayme.   [dizain 49]
>
> Avec le front serenant l'esperance,
> J'asseure l'Ame, & le Cœur obligez . . .   [dizain 45]

This is not to deny that such abstractions could be used in other
contexts for other purposes and that side by side with the
formalised use of abstractions in poetry there were contexts in
which the same figures had a more semantically important role
to play. After all we are quite accustomed to such situations
today, when many technical terms from diverse fields such as
psychology or economics are regularly employed in vague, non-
technical contexts for which they were never intended.

One could extend these comments on words such as *âme*,
esprit, and *sens* to Scève's use of the noun *Raison*. Once again I
would suggest that there are dangers in attempting to provide
too precise a definition of the term and in neglecting the long
tradition which lies behind it. For Saulnier *Raison* 'n'est

nullement, comme on pourrait le croire, une des puissances de l'homme: elle est bien son auxiliaire et peut venir en lui, mais reste extérieure à lui, essentiellement'. In this he is followed by Vernay, who writes: 'Pour Maurice Scève, la *raison* est en premier lieu ce principe extérieur à l'homme, mais venant en lui pour le diriger dans ses actes. Elle est la lumière qui dirige nos facultés vers leur objet respectif.'[21] Saulnier's view, however, is based on his reading of dizains 179 to 184. I have already discussed two of the poems in this group and I pointed out that in lines such as 'Quand pied a pied la Raison je costoye' from dizain 180 one finds one of the few examples of true allegory in the *Délie*. In such a context *Raison* appears quite naturally as a distinct character, an exterior force, rather than an internalized abstraction, but one cannot generalise on the basis of such an untypical example. Elsewhere in the *Délie*, *Raison* appears in the same contexts as the other abstract figures we have discussed and has a similarly colourless function. This is true in dizain 1, for example, which I have already quoted:

> Mon Basilisque avec sa poingnant' veue
> Perçant Corps, Cœur, & Raison despourveue . . .

An interesting example of Scève's use of the word *raison* occurs in dizain 439. He begins that poem with the line: 'Bien que raison soit nourrice de l'ame . . .' *Raison* is here a complete abstraction, but the presence of the noun *nourrice* reminds one that, underlying many of Scève's abstract relationships, there is the lost world of allegory in which those same relationships were once fully dramatised and humanised. Look, for example, at the following lines from Charles d'Orléans:

> Mort de moy! vous y jouez vous
> Avec Dame Merencolye!
> Mon cueur, vous faictes grant folye!
> C'est la nourice de Courroux.   [rondeau 194]

Saulnier misses the essential context, I think, when he attempts to define the word *ame* in the line from dizain 439. He quotes from Leone Ebreo ('L'anima è mezzo frà l'intelletto, e il corpo'), and he suggests that *ame* 'est parfois, presque au sens platoniste, une sorte d'intermédiaire entre le corps et l'intellect'.[22] This view seems to me too precise and too

restrictive, and I think Scève almost never provides the kind of
information which would be necessary for such an analytical
approach to the question of abstraction.

I have already suggested that abstract figures can be of
considerable value to a poet in a purely practical sense, and I
give two further examples in illustration. Both involve
translations from Italian into French. The first is taken from
Bourgouyn's verse translation (c. 1530) of Petrarch's *Trionfi*,
where one finds that a single line from the *Triumphus Mortis*:

> per ch'io lunga stagion cantai ed arsi

is expanded thus:

> Par lesquelz j'ay chanté en vers longue saison
> Et fuz ardant d'amour en l'aymant par raison . . .[23]

One may sympathise with the difficulties of the translator, but
such expansions are scarcely satisfactory. *Stagion* goes literally
into French as *saison*, and *raison* is then added as a mere rhyming
tool, which, through the largely meaningless phrase 'en
l'aymant par raison', dilutes and obscures all the natural
simplicity of the original. My second example is very similar. I
mentioned earlier (p. 33) the translation which Jean Marot made
of Serafino's poem beginning 'Se questo miser corpo t'abandona'.
In the opening lines of that translation we find another attempt
to expand on the original for purely practical purposes:

> Se questo miser corpo t'abandona
>   Inclita mia madonna, el cor ti resta
>   In cambio di mia fé . . .
> S'il est ainsi que ce corps t'abandonne,
> Amour commande & la raison ordonne
> Que je te laisse en gaige de ma foy
> Le cueur ja tien . . .

The second line of the Marot version is a complete invention,
simply providing a balanced pair of abstractions to accompany a
convenient rhyme. The use of such abstractions in tandem is
common all through the *Délie*:

> Sa grace asses, sans moy, luy peult donner
> Corps a ses faictz, & Ame a son hault nom.   [dizain 227]

> Raison au faict me rend souffle a la vie,
> Vertu au sens, & vigueur aux espritz.   [dizain 413]

While in dizain 424 Scève employs the technique in both the opening and closing lines of the poem:

De corps tresbelle & d'ame bellissime . . .   [l. 1]
Parfaicte au corps, & en l'ame accomplie.   [l. 10]

The use of this kind of device rarely leads to successful poetry, and this is especially true when the functional nature of the device is uppermost in the reader's mind. Thus I think the very angular separation that one finds in dizain 134, between what belongs to Délie's husband and what belongs to the poet, fails to impress:

A luy & Corps & Foy abandonna:
A moy le Cœur, & la chaste pensée.

Whereas there is much more warmth in Clément Marot's treatment of the same theme simply because he refers to the separation in a way that seems les mechanical:

Touchant son cueur, je l'ay en ma cordelle,
Et son Mary n'a sinon le Corps d'elle . . .[24]

Of course, Scève does not always employ his abstractions in combination, but even when used singly the words seldom come to life. In dizain 322, for example, the use of *ame* merely seems to distance the reader from the emotions of the poet, and this is a common phenomenon, as I suggested earlier:

Mais congnoissant soubz tes celestes mains
Estre mon ame heureusement traictée . . .

The use of an intermediary, standing between the reader and the poet, often makes it difficult to respond in anything other than an intellectual manner, and the modern reader may well be disconcerted by this apparent objectification of sentiment:

L'Ame craignant si dangereux loyer,
Se pert en moy, comme toute paoureuse . . .   [dizain 390]

or

Mon ame ainsi de son object pourveue
De tous mes sens me rend abandonné . . .   [dizain 443]

The reader may often feel that nothing is actually happening to the poet himself, and this impression is the direct result of the peculiar situation in which Scève's abstractions are placed, being neither completely autonomous figures nor sufficiently personalised so that they could function in a truly allegorical manner. Consider how much more dramatic is Ronsard's use of the word *ame* in the following lines:

> Sinope, baisez moy, non: ne me baisez pas,
>   Mais tirez moy le cueur de vostre douce halene.
>   Non: ne le tirez pas, mais hors de chaque vene
>   Sucez moy toute l'ame esparse entre vos bras.[25]

Or compare the famous lines from Marvell's 'To his Coy Mistress':

> And while thy willing Soul transpires
>   At every pore with instant Fires . . .   [ll. 35–6]

There is very little like this in the *Délie*. For Scève it would seem that abstractions have a largely functional role to play. They can provide both a time-honoured way of conveying emotional relationships in shorthand form and a practical solution to some of the problems of structure which the dizain presents. The words *ame*, *corps*, *esprit*, *cœur*, and *raison* appear more than three hundred times in the *Délie*, and, while any generalisations over so wide an area are inevitably open to question, I think it is fair to say that Scève's successes in the field of abstraction are very limited. Indeed I would maintain that it is Scève's reliance on the debris of the medieval abstract/allegorical tradition which principally accounts for the status he has acquired as a poet of talent who often produced fine lines but only occasionally fine poems. At this point we may conveniently move on to look at the new world of the Pléiade.

5   A new style of loving

The reader should now be in a good position to determine for himself the nature of the revolution which Ronsard and du Bellay brought to the world of traditional French love poetry. J. Tortel, in his *Poésies de Maurice Scève*, succinctly characterises the evolution which took place in the decade following the publication of the *Délie* when he writes: 'en ce qui concerne Scève, intervient l'existence du fait Ronsard: car si le Vendômois sut admirablement organiser sa publicité et celle de son école, il a aussi attiré la lumière parce qu'il a donné de l'air à la poésie.'[1] From the opening of sonnet of Ronsard's *Amours* (1552–3), or the opening sonnet of du Bellay's *Olive* (1549–50), we are in a quite different poetic tradition from any we have discussed so far. Of course it is easy to show that the revolution was not absolute. There are times when both Ronsard and du Bellay can sound just like Scève at his most conventional. Look at the ending of *Amours* 48, for example (the poem beginning 'Dame, depuis que la premiere fléche . . .'):

> Plus je l'apelle, & plus je le convie,
> Plus fait le sourd, & ne me répond point.

or the ending of *Amours* 12 ('J'espere & crains, je me tais & supplie'):

> Et pour aymer perdant toute puissance,
> Ne pouvant rien je fay ce que je puis.

Or look at the opening lines of *Olive* 28, which could have come from anywhere in the *Délie*:

> Ce que je sen', la langue ne refuse
> Vous decouvrir, quand suis de vous absent,
> Mais tout soudain que pres de moy vous sent,
> Elle devient & muette & confuse.

> Ainsi, l'espoir me promect & m'abuse:
> Moins pres je suis, quand plus je suis present . . .

Here we find ourselves still firmly within the old French courtly tradition, with its delight in dry paradox and its lack of imagery. But that is not really the point. However inferior Ronsard's *Amours* or du Bellay's *Olive* may be in relation to their later works, they are immeasurably superior to almost all the love poetry which had been written in France in the preceding two hundred years or so.

We may begin by looking at the first sonnet of the *Amours*:

> Qui voudra voyr comme un Dieu me surmonte,
>   Comme il m'assault, comme il se fait vainqueur,
>   Comme il r'enflamme, & r'englace mon cuœur,
>   Comme il reçoit un honneur de ma honte,
> Qui voudra voir une jeunesse prompte
>   A suyvre en vain l'object de son malheur,
>   Me vienne voir: il voirra ma douleur,
>   Et la rigueur de l'Archer qui me donte.
> Il cognoistra combien la raison peult
>   Contre son arc, quand une foys il veult
>   Que nostre cuœur son esclave demeure:
> Et si voirra que je suis trop heureux,
>   D'avoir au flanc l'aiguillon amoureux,
>   Plein du venin dont il fault que je meure.

It will immediately be objected that there is nothing very brilliant about this poem, and indeed the theme in entirely conventional. One notes the antithesis of the icy fire in l. 3 or the paradox of the unhappy lover cherishing his suffering in ll. 12–13. But there are two important things to notice about this sonnet, however banal its argument may be. In the first place we are in the presence of a well-defined poetic personality. We may find that personality somewhat annoying, adolescent, presumptuous, and narcissistic, but the very fact that we can sense a distinct individual behind the poetry is in itself significant. It is something we encounter rarely in French love poetry before Ronsard. I have no very clear idea what Machaut was like, or Chartier, or even Scève, though I have spent many hours over the past ten years or so reading their work. With Ronsard you are keenly aware of a personality after a few minutes' casual browsing. Of course you may modify your ideas later and you may realise that the poetic personality does not perhaps correspond to anything outside the context of the particular poem you happen to be reading. That does not matter. It is the driving force of a dominant personality which

alone allows the poet to carry conviction in some of his finest
lyrics, and there is no better illustration of the fact than in the
opening of the following sonnet from the *Sonets pour Helene*,
bk. II:

> Quand vous serez bien vieille, au soir à la chandelle,
> Assise aupres du feu, devidant & filant,
> Direz, chantant mes vers, en vous esmerveillant,
> Ronsard me celebroit du temps que j'estois belle.   [No. 24]

In the face of such assurance so many poems belonging to the
preceding French tradition fade into insignificance. Though the
comparison is in some ways not a fair one—for we have seen
that Scève can produce love lyrics of the highest quality—it is
interesting to set the following lines from dizain 381 of the *Délie*
against the opening quatrain of Ronsard's sonnet:

> Je sens en moy la vilté de la crainte
> Movoir l'horreur a mon indignité
> Parqui la voix m'est en la bouche estaincte
> Devant les piedz de ta divinité.

Scève can indeed do better than this, but the lines are not
untypical of the sort of poetry which was popular in France
over an extremely long period of time. There is very little here
which could be called personality, and the whole tradition from
which the lines derive seems remote and inaccessible to the
modern reader.

For those who, quite wrongly in my opinion, blame the evil
genius of Petrarch for everything that they think is wrong with
the French tradition of love poetry, there is something
reassuring in the confident attack which Ronsard makes on the
Canzoniere in the *Nouvelle Continuation des Amours*. Petrarch, he
says, claimed to have loved Laura for thirty years, but that is not
an example which he is keen to follow. In any case, Ronsard
wonders whether Petrarch could really have been so stupid as to
have loved one woman for so long, unless, of course, their
relationship had been a thorough-going sexual one:

> . . . Petrarque sur moy
> N'avoit authorité pour me donner sa loy,
> Ny à ceux qui viendroient apres luy, pour les faire
> Si long temps amoureux sans s'en pouvoir deffaire:
> Luy mesme ne fut tel: car à voir son escrit
> Il estoit esveillé d'un trop gentil esprit

Pour estre sot trente ans, abusant sa jeunesse,
Et sa Muse, au giron d'une seule maitresse:
Ou bien il jouissoit de sa Laurette, ou bien
Il estoit un grand fat d'aymer sans avoir rien,
Ce que je ne puis croire, aussi n'est-il croiable:
Non, il en jouissoit, puis l'a faitte admirable,
"Chaste, divine, sainte: aussi tout amant doit
"Loüer celle de qui jouissance il reçoit:
"Car celuy qui la blasme apres la jouissance
"N'est homme, mais d'un Tygre il a prins sa naissance.

> [*Nouvelle Continuation des Amours*, No. 42, ll. 41 ff.]

The attack is crude and manifestly unfair. Petrarch, we are
assured, only wrote in lofty terms of Laura because she had been
his mistress; if you are a proper gentleman then you are duty-
bound to call a woman 'chaste, divine, sainte' once you have
made love to her. But of course Ronsard did not always talk of
Petrarch in these terms. In *Le Bocage* of 1554, published two
year before the *Nouvelle Continuation des Amours*, he still writes
approvingly of 'l'art de bien Petrarquiser'[2] (in the 'Elegie à
Cassandre'). He tells Cassandre that since the king has comman-
ded him to abandon lyric poetry in order to sing the praises of
the French royal line,[3] his hopes of one day rivalling the
'Tuscan lyre' are now gone:

Donques en vain je me paissois d'espoir
De faire un jour à la Thuscane voir
Que nôtre France, autant qu'elle, est heureuse
A souspirer une pleinte amoureuse . . .

> [*Le Bocage*, No. 13, ll. 19 ff.]

So it is clear that in Ronsard's attack on Petrarch there was more
than a little jealousy in the face of the enormous prestige and
authority which the *Canzoniere* had achieved in the field of lyric
poetry. But doubtless it was an attack which had to be made at
some stage. We have seen that the courtly tradition was
potentially capable of carrying a very wide range of attitudes to
love, both sensuous and platonic. But if we look at the *Jardin*,
which gives a fair impression of the way the courtly movement
developed in France, we find that the poems tend to be divided
between those which express the dullest and most unerotic
aspects of the courtly world, and those which are so obvious and
so natural in their approach to sexuality that they could not be
said to belong to that world at all. We have also seen that the

Petrarchan tradition was in many ways indistinguishable from
the debris of the old French courtly movement, and I think that
but for the Pléiade its effect might well have been to legitimise
all that was worst in late medieval poetry by providing a
framework of superficial novelty. No later poet ever matched
what was best in Petrarch, whereas the superficial aspects of his
verse were readily imitable by anyone with the minimum of
talent. Thus the attack on Petrarch, however unfair it may have
been, had a healthy side to it, and it was something which
needed to be done by a poet who was greater than Antoine
Héroët, the author of the *Parfaicte Amye*, who as early as 1542
had voiced his own misgivings about the superficiality of the
Petrarchan tradition. He refers to:

> Touts les escripts et larmoyants autheurs,
> Tout le Petrarcque et ses imitateurs,
> Qui de souspirs et de froydes querelles
> Remplissent l'air en parlant aux estoilles . . .[4]

Whatever Ronsard's motives may have been, he had the talent
and the force of personality to give back to serious love poetry a
proper emotional and erotic range. He was able to depart from
the role of the traditional passive and colourless lover to which
the majority of the followers of the Petrarchan/courtly
movement had relegated themselves, and this unmistakable
example of emotional independence was of considerable
symbolic importance.

The second point which I would like to make in connection
with the opening sonnet of the *Amours* is an aesthetic one.
Desonay has pointed out that this opening poem has a
movement which is characteristic of a large number of
Ronsard's sonnets, and he comments: 'C'est le mouvement
mélodique qui emporte d'une seule coulée les deux quatrains et
les deux tercets.'[5] The attention which Ronsard habitually pays
to the melodic continuity of his verse is closely linked to his
preferance for very simple types of formal construction, and in
both respects his poetry offers an extraordinary contrast to that
of the majority of his predecessors. Nothing could be simpler
than the arrangement of *Amours* 1:

> Qui voudra voyr / Qui voudra voir
> Me vienne voir: il voirra / Il cognoistra /
> Et si voirra /

A poet such as Scève, on the other hand, seldom shows a sustained interest in matters of this kind. The structure of many of his dizains is extremely fluid and I doubt whether he was ever much concerned with lyric beauty for its own sake, unless, of course, it was of the kind which we are no longer able to appreciate. Consider the following lines which conclude dizain 94 of the *Délie*:

> Ainsi Amour, perdu a nous, rendit
> Vexation, qui donne entendement.

This scarcely seems like poetry at all. The four syllables of *Vexation* and the four of *entendement* leave little room for anything else in the final line, and as I read it the rhythm is that of prose, rather than poetry. Scève is content to break up the individual line into any number of smaller units and to subdivide the whole poem in a variety of different ways. As Guidici puts it, 'si può dire che Scève abbia utilizzato quasi tutte le maniere in cui può suddividersi una composizione di dieci versi'.[6] In the *Délie* we find numerous poems which wander in a seemingly aimless fashion, following the vagaries of the poet's thought processes. I can think of nothing which is further from the spirit of Ronsard's sonnets than the following dizain of the *Délie*:

> Me desaymant par la severité
> De mon estrange, & propre jugement,
> Qui me fait veoir, & estre en verité
> Non meritant si doulx soulagement,
> Comme celluy, dont pend l'abregement
> De mes travaux me bienheurantz ma peine,
> Je m'extermine, & en si grande hayne
> De mes deffaultz j'aspire a la merveille
> D'un si hault bien, que d'une mesme alaine
> A mon labeur le jour, & la nuict veille.

> [No. 384]

This syntactic and rhythmic fluidity is characteristic of much late medieval verse and Ronsard's reaction against it is extremely significant. For the future of the French language lay quite clearly in the direction which Ronsard had taken, and that is why his poetry seems so much more modern to us than the poetry of the *Délie*. As Weber puts it: 'alors que le français tend dès le XVIème siècle à évoluer vers un ordre grammatical plus rigoureux, Scève reste sur ce point fidèle à la tradition antique.'[7]

The comparisons which I have been making between the
opening sonnet of the *Amours* and the poetry which preceded it
could be extended to du Bellay's *Olive*. The latter collection
first appeared in 1549 when it contained a mere fifty sonnets. A
second edition was published a year later and the number of
sonnets had by then increased to one hundred and fifteen. This is
how du Bellay begins:

> Je ne quiers pas la fameuse couronne,
> Sainct ornement du Dieu au chef doré,
> Ou que du Dieu aux Indes adoré
> Le gay chapeau la teste m'environne.
>
> Encores moins veulx-je que lon me donne
> Le mol rameau en Cypre decoré:
> Celuy qui est d'Athenes honoré,
> Seul je le veulx, & le Ciel me l'ordonne.
>
> O tige heureux, que la sage Déesse
> En sa tutelle & garde a voulu prendre,
> Pour faire honneur à son sacré autel!
>
> Orne mon chef, donne moy hardiesse
> De te chanter, qui espere te rendre
> Egal un jour au Laurier immortel.

This poem is no more striking to the modern reader than the
opening sonnet of the *Amours*, and yet its significance can be
measured in very similar terms. Du Bellay consciously and
openly sets himself the task of competing with Petrarch in the
field of lyric poetry. He looks forward to the day when his olive
and Petrarch's laurel will be seen in the same terms, and this
declaration of intent cannot but draw our attention to his work.
Most critics would agree that du Bellay's best poetry is not to be
found in the *Olive*, but it is clear that he possessed, from the very
beginning of his career, a firm idea of what it means to be a
poet, and that is a considerable step forward. The desire for
glory can be a very powerful spur to creative activity, and this is
as true of the glory that the poet seeks for himself as of the glory
he seeks (or pretends to seek) for his beloved. So many poets
before du Bellay seem to have little idea of why they are
composing poetry at all. They claim they are unhappy, or else
they cherish the thought of softening their implacable mistress
by their verse so that she will abandon herself to their 'honest

desires'. This approach can be successful on a small scale, but the
demands of a sequence are rather more strenuous. In the
opening sonnets of the *Olive* and the *Amours* we are immediately
made aware of a poetic personality; to put it crudely you could
say that both du Bellay and Ronsard begin on a note of self-
advertisement, and however much you may dislike this, it is, at
least, a beginning. If you then turn to the opening dizain of
Scève's collection, the differences are at once apparent. This
dizain provides no evidence to suggest that the poet has any
clear underlying purpose in composing the long sequence on
which we are about to embark. It is a poem which simply
describes the act of falling in love in terms that are completely
traditional:

> Voicy (ô paour d'agreables terreurs)
> Mon Basilisque avec sa poingnant' veue
> Perçant Corps, Cœur, & Raison despourveue,
> Vint penetrer en l'Ame de mon Ame.

The image of the basilisk is a common one. We find it in the
poetry of Jean Molinet (1435–1507), for example:

> Son oeul comme ung fier basilicque
> Occist mon cœur de son regard.[8]

And the technique whereby love is presented as an advancing
force, affecting in turn the poet's body, heart, reason, and soul,
is, as we have seen, no less traditional in late French medieval
poetry. There is no sense that the poet has engaged in some kind
of poetic commitment, that he is aware of himself as an
individual interpreter of a particular experience. There is
nothing like the powerful appeal of the opening sonnet of the
Canzoniere, in which we are brought to the realisation that
everything we are about to read is symbolic of the futility of
earthly things and that love of a woman belongs to the same
category as the love engendered by any material and transitory
object. Scève's opening dizain could easily have been placed
elsewhere in the collection, with little loss to the overall
structure of the sequence.

The question of love leads one naturally to enquire about the
nature of the women who are celebrated in the various
collections we have been discussing. Critics often point out that
the women who are ostensibly the subjects of sequences rarely

seem to possess a very strongly-marked personality. They all
appear to be alike in their beauty and their lofty disdain. As De
Sanctis suggests, 'Laura è una Dea, non è ancora una donna',
while Chamard dismisses Olive as 'un prétexte à beaux vers'.⁹
This is not really the point, however. In a collection of love
poems written by a man it is inevitably the personality of the
man which will be of prime interest, and if there is little to
distinguish Laura from Olive or Délie on objective grounds, the
impact made by the different poets in the pursuit of their
beloved is quite distinctive in each case. Women are the
catalysts in all sequences, they provide the initial impetus
towards self-examination, and they offer an emotional and
artistic centre from which the poet can proceed to discuss
anything he wishes. As J. H. Whitfield puts it, 'it is Petrarch,
more than Laura, who is the centre of the *Rime*': for the main
interest in the *Canzoniere* is 'the conflict generated within the
mind of Petrarch. To it doubtless Laura is essential, but it is, to
use a language Dante might have used, as accident to
substance.'¹⁰ Rather than attempting to define the shadowy
character of the women who appear before us in the various
sequences, I shall try to show that it is the poet's reaction to
these women which provides the principal source of interest.
We may look first at sonnet 50 from the *Amours*:

> Mon dieu, mon dieu, que ma maistresse est belle!
>   Soit que j'admire ou ses yeus, mes seigneurs,
>   Ou de son front les dous-graves honneurs,
>   Ou l'Orient de sa levre jumelle.
> Mon dieu, mon dieu, que ma dame est cruelle!
>   Soit qu'un raport rengrege mes douleurs,
>   Soit qu'un depit parannise mes pleurs,
>   Soit qu'un refus mes plaïes renouvelle.
> Ainsi le miel de sa douce beauté
>   Nourrit mon cœur: ainsi sa cruauté
>   D'aluine amere enamere ma vie.
> Ainsi repeu d'un si divers repas,
>   Ores je vi, ores je ne vi pas
>   Egal au sort des freres d'Œbalie.

The spirit of this poem is quite foreign to the *Canzoniere*, or to
the *Olive*, or to the *Délie*. It is stamped with Ronsard's own
particular brand of aggressive self-assurance. The poet is
describing the sufferings he experiences in love, but it is evident

that he has no desire to withdraw into the background to
meditate on his fate in silence. The themes he introduces are
those which had dominated love poetry for hundreds of years
and yet the treatment is entirely different from anything I have
come across in the earlier French tradition, a point which
emphasises once again how important it is to consider stylistic as
well as thematic criteria in any discussion of sources and
influence within the context of the love lyric.

Ronsard's mistress is hard-hearted, beautiful, and as much in
control of her lover's destiny as any courtly lady ever was. But
the complex and ambiguous language of the courtly tradition
has disappeared and left scarcely a trace behind. No one could
misunderstand what the poet has to say. There is no devious talk
of *vouloir* and *volonté*, *bien* and *mal*, nothing very subtle behind
the images of the bitter-sweet nature of love. The poet is
suffering a living death like all his predecessors, but he is not
interested in making anything more than a dramatic statement
of this position. If Ronsard could be said to have 'donné de l'air
à la poésie', this was achieved largely through a process of
simplification, on the levels of syntax, vocabulary, and
construction. One of the basic truths about the *Amours* is that
they are extraordinarily easy to read in comparison with much
of the love poetry which preceded them. You can spend quite a
long time elucidating some of the poems in the *Jardin*, and there
are numerous dizains from the *Délie* that still await a satisfactory
interpretation. But you can read the *Amours* at a reasonable
speed with the help of a proper glossary. The sonnet which we
have been discussing would no doubt have appeared very
unsubtle to many of the courtly practitioners and indeed it is in
no sense a great poem. But it contains all the elements which
were to enable Ronsard to modernise the French lyric tradition.
In his most famous poems Ronsard is never subtle in the old
sense. His achievement was to give to the figure of the
lover/poet a personality, something which makes us convinced
that we are dealing with real people in real situations, and
though we may be quite aware of the extent to which this
impression is an illusory one, the advance is of enormous
significance. Look at the following sonnet, one of the most
famous from bk. II of the *Sonets pour Helene*:

Ces longues nuicts d'hyver, où la Lune ocieuse
Tourne si lentement son char tout à l'entour,

Où le Coq si tardif nous annonce le jour,
Où la nuict semble un an à l'ame soucieuse:
  Je fusse mort d'ennuy sans ta forme douteuse,
Qui vient par une feinte alleger mon amour,
Et faisant, toute nue, entre mes bras sejour,
Me pipe doucement d'une joye menteuse.
  Vraye tu es farouche, & fiere en cruauté:
De toy fausse on jouyst en toute privauté.
Pres ton mort je m'endors, pres de luy je repose:
  Rien ne m'est refusé. Le bon sommeil ainsi
Abuse par le faux mon amoureux souci.
S'abuser en amour n'est pas mauvaise chose.

[No. 23]

It is a superb poem, but it is not subtle in the sense that the
reader would need to work at it for a while in order to
disentangle the argument. The subtlety lies on an emotional
level, in the seeming paradox which is stated in the final line.
The poet evokes the torment of the long winter nights which he
has to endure alone and then suddenly we are aware of the
presence of his beloved, not in the shape of some allegorical
figure such as *Doulce Pensée*, but as a real woman who is entirely
human and who comes to offer him all the erotic consolation a
man could desire. *Doulce Pensée* has exactly the same function to
perform in the *Roman de la Rose*, but, because we are now so
completely divorced from the allegorical tradition, Ronsard's
sonnet appears much more powerful in the way it is able to
dramatize the universal experience of wish fulfilment. The lady
who comes to grant the favours she has refused in the real world
may be as cruel, or indeed as colourless, as any of her courtly
perdecessors, but this does not matter since the role she is called
upon to play is in no sense an individual one. Her function is
simply to act as a stimulus to the imagination. For the poet and
the reader she is the embodiment of everything that is most
desirable, and the whole force of the poem derives from the
realization that it is only in a world of fantasy that she would
ever offer herself with such directness and simplicity. That is
why the poet is able to carry conviction when he concludes that
to deceive oneself in love is not necessarily such a bad thing.
The pleasures he has experienced are not faded representations
of something more real. On the contrary, they are pleasures
which he has created alone, and which are thus irrecoverable

elsewhere. Any woman would have sufficed to set the poem in motion. But we must be convinced that in real life she would have been cold and unresponsive, for there is a powerful element of revenge in all compositions of this type, and if the poem is to succeed the reader must be involved as a willing accomplice. The point is well illustrated by Donne's 'The Apparition':

> When by thy scorn, O murderess, I am dead,
> And that thou think'st thee free
> From all solicitation from me,
> Then shall my ghost come to thy bed,
> And thee, feigned vestal, in worse arms shall see;
> Then thy sick taper will begin to wink,
> And he, whose thou art then, being tired before,
> Will, if thou stir, or pinch to wake him, think
>   Thou call'st for more,
> And in false sleep will from thee shrink,
> And then poor aspen wretch, neglected thou
> Bathed in a cold quicksilver sweat wilt lie
>   A verier ghost than I . . .

It is strange when one reflects that the lady's only crime was a disinclination to be seduced. Indeed the fate of women in love poetry written by men is often not a very happy one.

It is perhaps worth pointing out once again how simple Ronsard's sonnets are in their formal construction. The sonnet we have just been considering from the *Sonets pour Helene* is a little more complex in this respect than *Amours* 50, but then it could scarcely have been less so. The architecture of the individual poem is in both cases very clearly defined, and we find the same attention to formal neatness in the majority of the sonnets in the *Olive*. Very often the structure of the poem is underlined in what seems to us the most obvious way, by the repetition of individual words or phrases. Thus in *Amours* 50 we find that only three lines begin with words which are not repeated elsewhere in the poem, and the basic division between quatrains and tercets is clearly indicated by the repetition of 'Mon dieu, mon dieu' and 'Ainsi'. In *Olive* 7 we find a similar technique:

> De grand' beauté ma Déesse est si pleine,
> Que je ne voy' chose au monde plus belle.

Soit que le front je voye, ou les yeulx d'elle,
Dont la clarté saincte me guyde & meine:

Soit ceste bouche, ou souspire une halaine
Qui les odeurs des Arabes excelle:
Soit ce chef d'or, qui rendroit l'estincelle
Du beau Soleil honteuse, obscure & vaine:

Soient ces coustaux d'albastre, & main polie,
Qui mon cœur serre, enferme, estreinct & lie,
Bref, ce que d'elle on peult ou voir ou croyre,

Tout est divin, celeste, incomparable:
Mais j'ose bien me donner ceste gloyre,
Que ma constance est trop plus admirable.

This is in some ways a rather banal poem of praise, typical of a
number of the sonnets in the *Olive*. There is no doubt that du
Bellay was able to play the role of the old-fashioned lover with
much greater ease than Ronsard, for, as A. Gendre puts it: 'Si
l'on peut dire que Ronsard ne fut pas sourd aux appels d'un
amour uniquement spirituel . . . on constate que ses désirs de
possession charnelle, si nombreux et si constants, rangent le
Vendômois dans le clan des amoureaux à qui leur instinct suffit.'[11]
In the *Olive* we do not find that kind of erotic tension which is
characteristic of many of Ronsard's finest poems. All still seems
rather too controlled and artificial on the physical plane. Du
Bellay sets forth the various qualities of his beloved: she is
perfect in every respect and he is totally under her spell. Her
breath is sweeter than all the perfumes of Arabia and the
brilliance of her golden hair would make the sun envious. She is
a goddess and incomparable. Then the poet concludes, in a
somewhat laboured fashion, that there is something even more
admirable than all this, and that is the constancy with which he
serves his divine beloved. If one feels that it would have been
more interesting to have met Cassandre than Olive, that is
entirely the fault of du Bellay's approach to his subject, for I
think we find it difficult to respond to love poetry which seems
so consciously unerotic. But even so banal a poem as *Olive* 7
reveals an assured handling of the sonnet form, and the
simplicity of construction, which is underlined throughout by
the repetition of 'Soit/Soient', is also characteristic of the best
sonnets in the sequence, such as *Olive* 83, the famous poem

beginning 'Deja la nuit en son parc amassoit / Un grand troupeau d'etoiles vagabondes'.

It is easy at this distance to take the introduction of the sonnet for granted and to forget that it was one of the most important events in the whole history of French love poetry. Of course other poets had employed the sonnet form in France before du Bellay: Marot, Saint-Gelais, Marguerite de Navarre, Scève, and Peletier du Mans had all preceded him in this respect. The question as to who was first is, as ever, a somewhat unrewarding one, but in Weber's edition of the *Amours* there is the following reasonable summary of the situation: 'C'est à Marot que l'on doit probablement le premier sonnet français publié en 1538. Il reste possible que Mellin de Saint-Gelais ait composé bien avant, vers 1533 un sonnet qui ne sera édité que beaucoup plus tard' (p. v). But if du Bellay was not the first to employ the sonnet form in France, he was certainly the first to produce a sequence of love poems in sonnets, and the significance of this can hardly be overemphasised. The *Olive* effectively established the sonnet as the only form which could be used for a long series of poems about love, and if one thinks of the enormously long tradition of ballades, rondeaux, and 'autres telles episseries' which lies behind du Bellay,[12] and which the *Délie* had done so little to alter, the innovations introduced by the *Olive* can be seen in their proper perspective. The techniques of repetition to underline the structure of the sonnet, which we have observed in the work of Ronsard and du Bellay from the time of their earliest compositions, may seem obvious to a modern reader, but they clearly had a vital role to play in the formal revolution which was taking place. The dizain, a form which never really possessed a well-defined structure and which almost certainly derived from the ballade, offered Scève the possiblity of dividing his poems in many different ways, and we have seen that he took full advantage of the fact. We find dizains arranged 6+4 and 4+6, 4+2+4, 4+4+2, 8+2, and indeed there are sixty-six examples of dizains with no division at all.[13] There is no doubt that this formal fluidity suited Scève's temperament very well, but from a modern point of view the movement towards the fixed structure of the sonnet was a highly desirable one, both in aesthetic terms and in the way it led to a greater precision in the presentation of the argument.

If one looks at the large number of sonnets by Ronsard and du

Bellay which are built around one or two key words or phrases,
and then compares the results with Scève's techniques in the
Délie, the differences are immediately striking. Look, for
example, at *Olive* 50, which has five lines beginning with 'Si',
or at No. 55, with nine lines beginning in 'O', or No. 46, with
three lines beginning with 'Quel' and four with 'Qui', or No.
96 in which there are thirteen lines introduced by 'Ny'. Look at
Amours 47, where we find both quatrains and both tercets
beginning with 'Je veus mourir', No. 49, which has eight lines
beginning with 'Ni', or No. 55, which has eight lines
introduced by 'O'. The effect of this technique obviously varies
from sonnet to sonnet, but its relationship to the formal
structure of the poem is clearly established. Scève's use of
repetition in this way is, on the other hand, extremely limited,
and is generally confined to one or two lines only. The sustained
movement of the opening of dizain 265 is quite uncharacteristic
of the majority of the poems in the *Délie*:

> Tous temps je tumbe entre espoir, & desir:
> Tousjours je suis meslé de doubte, & craincte:
> Tous lieux me sont ennuy, & desplaisir:
> Tout libre faict m'est esclave contraincte . . .

Even the technique of apostrophe which is so common in the
sonnets of Ronsard and du Bellay is rarely used by Scève, and is
never sustained over more than a few lines:

> O ans, ô moys, sepmaines, jours, & heures,
> O intervalle, ô minute, ô moment . . .
>
>   [dizain 114]

The general aim of a sonnet by Ronsard or du Bellay is to
convey the argument with simplicity and precision. There is
almost always an effort to sustain the movement of the lines
across the whole poem, and to this end all the details of the
argument are subjected. In Scève's dizains we frequently have
the impression that he is determined to say whatever he likes in
the manner which he finds most convenient, and questions of
overall structure often seem to be of secondary importance. The
comparison could be extended into the field of imagery. For in
Ronsard's sonnets the images too are normally integrated fully
into the structure of the poem, whereas this is much more rarely
the case with Scève. If one looks at *Amours* 60 one finds that the
whole substance of the poem is concerned with the traditional

comparison between the lover and the hunted stag. The
comparison is introduced by the phrase 'Comme un chevreuil'
at the beginning of the first quatrain, and completed by a formal
'Ainsi j'alloy' at the beginning of the final tercet. When Scève
uses the same theme in dizain 46 of the *Délie* the effect is totally
different. Eight lines of the poem are given over to an abstract
discussion concerning the impossibility of ever escaping from
the bitter-sweetness of love, and the two lines given to the
image of the stag (ll. 7–8) appear simply as a passing illustration
of this abstract debate. Scève's area of interest is quite clear. He
shows no desire to develop the details of the image, nor is any
direct comparison made of the 'Comme . . . ainsi' variety. In this
respect I think it is clear that Scève's practice is quite in keeping
with his time, and that Ronsard's approach is distinctively new.

This brings me back to the question of abstraction which I
have raised so many times during the course of this book. I have
tried to show that the greatest contribution which Ronsard and
du Bellay made to French love poetry was to free it from its
traditional abstract preoccupations. If we compare even the
most banal of the sonnets from the *Amours* with the dizain by
Saint-Gelais that I quoted earlier, it is easy to see the progress
which had been made by 1552–53:

> Si la beauté qui vous rend si aimable,
> N'estoit pareille à mon affection,
> Elle seroit incertaine et muable,
> Et je serois hors de subjection;
> Mais comme seule elle a perfection,
> Aussi parfaicte est ma vive estincelle.
> L'une est céleste, et l'autre est éternelle,
> L'une est sans feu, l'autre sans cruauté:
> Telle beauté fait l'amour estre belle,
> Et tel amour aimable la beauté.[14]

This is totally familiar. The abstract vocabulary, the absence of
imagery, the totally intellectual approach to the question of
love, the arid delight in paradox and precious comparisons.
French love poetry might well have continued in this fashion
for many years, had it not been for the advent of the Pléiade.
Du Bellay's Olive may not have been a very exciting creature,
but at least she exists in a way that can be visualised, she is
something more than the outcome of abstract speculation.

Compare the second sonnet of the *Olive* with the second dizain of the *Délie*. Olive can perhaps even now stir a little enthusiasm:

> Ell' prist son teint des beaux lyz blanchissans,
> Son chef de l'or, ses deux levres des rozes,
> Et du soleil ses yeux resplandissans . . .

At least there is something to build on here, and with a trace of sensuality Ronsard might have made her almost human. But it is difficult to see what Délie has to offer to succeeding generations:

> Le Naturant par ses haultes Idées
> Rendit de soy la Nature admirable.
> Par les vertus de sa vertu guidées
> S'esvertua en œuvre esmerveillable.
>   Car de tout bien, voyre es Dieux desirable,
> Parfeit un corps en sa parfection,
> Mouvant aux Cieulx telle admiration,
> Qu'au premier œil mon ame l'adora . . .

In moving away from this kind of abstract presentation, Ronsard and du Bellay made a far greater use of concrete details drawn from the natural world than any of their predecessors had done. Weber overstates the true position, but he draws attention to this important phenomenon when he writes: 'pour les poètes de la Pléïade . . . l'essentiel ne sera plus le sentiment, mais le tableau à décrire ou l'effet esthétique à tirer de la fusion de la femme aimée avec les grandes forces cosmiques qui animent l'univers.'[15] Many of the poems in the *Amours* and the *Olive* are too slight to merit this sort of comment, but it is true to say that Ronsard and du Bellay have a natural tendency to describe their emotional reactions with reference to the visual world, whereas their predecessors were much more interested in analysing their feelings in terms of the traditional vocabulary of allegory and abstraction. Because of the way in which the European tradition of love poetry has developed, we are now very much more sympathetic to the former approach than to the latter. We are more willing to accept the banality of a glorious morning 'Kissing with golden face the meadows green'[16] than we are to accept the most complex, and even perhaps the most subtle, productions of the medieval abstract tradition.

  E. R. Curtius makes a number of interesting points about the medieval attitude to nature. He writes, 'Medieval descriptions of nature are not meant to represent reality', and earlier, 'The

medieval poet does not invoke nature, he enumerates its
component parts, and does so according to the principle, "The
more the better!" '17 Of course, like all generalisations, these are
in need of some qualification. Medieval poets were certainly
capable of responding to nature in as realistic a fashion as any
later writers. The following ballade by Charles d'Orléans
illustrates the point very well:

> Yver fait champs et arbres vieulx,
> Leurs barbes de neige blanchir,
> Et est si froit, ort et pluieux,
> Qu'emprés le feu couvient croupir.
> On ne peut hors des huis yssir . . .

[No. 79]

But the points which Curtius makes are valid none the less.
There is in much medieval poetry a very linear approach to the
recording of natural details. One can see this in the *Song of
Roland*, for instance, in lines such as the following which occur
from time to time in the course of the narrative: 'Hault sunt li
pui e mult halt les arbres' [l. 2271]. And this tendency is
characteristic of much early sixteenth-century poetry also. Look
at the following lines from the poem entitled 'A la louange de la
forest' by Eustorg de Beaulieu:

> En la Forest a mainte chose.
> En la Forest on se repose.
> En la Forest faict beau chasser,
> Beau chanter, beau le temps passer . . .18

A modern reader would conclude that there is not much feeling
for nature here, but it is clear that these formal inventories were
a source of delight to contemporary readers. There is something
very reassuring about convention, and when one considers that
medieval man was so much more obviously at the mercy of the
elements than modern man, it is easy to sympathise with the
stylised descriptions of natural scenes which one encounters at
every turn. It seems that the best thing that could have happened
to you in the medieval world was to have been alive and well
on one of those eternally beautiful spring days which form the
prelude to so many of the love songs of the period:

> Pluye d'avril et rousee de may,
> Prez verdoyans et gracieux bocage,
> Jardin fleury de roses et de glay,

Merles, mauvis, rossignolet sauvage,
Vrais amoureux qui d'amours avez gaige
Venez oyr la doulceur de ma dame,
Qui doulcement d'ung amoureux langaige
Son doulx servant et son amy me clame.

[Jardin, fo cxi]

Of course we must not expect to find in the work of the Pléiade an immediate and complete break with tradition. Grahame Castor points out that du Bellay has almost nothing to say about the relationship between the poet and nature in the whole of the *Deffence*,[19] and indeed in both the *Olive* and the *Amours* there are numerous poems which are only slightly less conventional in their approach to nature than the sort of poems we have been considering above. But the general direction in which French poetry was evolving is unmistakable. As early as the *Olive* we find the almost total abandonment of the sort of abstract combinations which had been so popular in the poetry of late medieval France. Lines such as the following from *Olive* 4 are quite uncharacteristic of the sequence as a whole:

Et que tes yeux, à ceulx qui te contemplent,
Cœur, corps, espirit, sens, ame & vouloir emblent . . .

And in place of these abstractions we tend to find, in however banal a form, the refreshing presence of the natural world. There could be nothing more conventional than the theme of *Amours* 169, but the treatment already looks forward to the richly evocative sonnets of Ronsard's later years:

Or que le ciel, or que la terre est pleine
   De glaz, de graille esparse en tous endrois,
   Et que l'horreur des plus frigoreux mois
   Fait herisser les cheveux de la plaine,
Or que le vent, qui mutin se promeine,
   Rompt les rochers, & desplante les bois,
   Et que la mer redoublant ses abois,
   Contre les bordz sa plus grand rage ameine,
Amour me brusle, & l'hyver froidureux,
   Qui gele tout, de mon feu chaleureux
   Ne gele point l'ardeur, qui tousjours dure:
Voyez, Amantz, comme je suis traitté,
   Je meurs de froid au plus chault de l'Esté,
   Et de chaleur au cuœur de la froidure.

The poet is suffering from the eternal effects of the icy fire, but the two quatrains do far more than simply prepare the reader for the introduction of that theme in l. 9. They reveal an independent interest in nature for its own sake, and Ronsard is led to develop a number of images which are only vaguely related to the specific emotions he claims to feel. As so very often it is the treatment of a theme, rather than the nature of the theme itself, which is of primary significance.

What role do Petrarch and Petrarchism have to play in the formal and aesthetic evolution we have been observing? This is scarcely the place to embark on the enormous topic of Pléiade Petrarchism, but one thing at least should be clear by now. If you wish to show that Petrarchism was indeed a major force in sixteenth-century French love poetry, its presence must be linked to some major change in poetic technique, and you do not find one until the advent of the Pléiade. We know much of the *Olive* was dependent on the Italian tradition. Du Bellay has only to begin a sonnet with the words 'Sus, chaulx soupirs, allez à ce froid cœur' (*Olive*, 67), and we are immediately in the world of the *Canzoniere*: 'Ite, caldi sospiri, al freddo core'. Before the *Olive* I do not think there is more than a superficial element of Petrarchism in France, and there is certainly no evidence to suggest that Italian poetry was exerting any revolutionary influence on the traditions which French love poetry had followed for so long. With the *Olive* it seems to me that a change is immediately apparent, even if the results were not as impressive as they were to be in Ronsard's later poetry. And we know that Ronsard was extremely keen to monitor du Bellay's activities in the field of Italian verse. A copy of the highly influential two-volume anthology of Italian poetry published by Gabriel Giolito has survived with annotations in Ronsard's hand.[20] R. Lebègue has examined these annotations and concludes that Ronsard was anxious above all to record the sources which du Bellay had already drawn on for the *Olive*: 'surtout il note les sources de l'*Olive*. Pourquoi? Parce qu'il n'est pas le premier poète français qui compose un recueil de sonnets amoureux ... Aussi prend-il soin de dépister les imitations de Du Bellay, afin de ne pas marcher sur ses brisées, et d'apporter à la poésie française des nouveautés.'[21] This conscious desire to be different is one of the most powerful elements in the poetry of Ronsard. It is, I think, something which is much more clearly expressed through his poetic technique than through any fundamental change in the thematic content of his verse, and if the feeling of *amour courtois* is indeed a universal one, this should in no way surprise us. When Ronsard writes, in *Amours* 11:

Que dois je faire? Amour me faict errer,
  Si haultement que je n'ose esperer
  De son salut que la desesperance . . .

we do not need to be told, as we inevitably will be, that the theme of hopeless hope was one that Petrarch and his Italian followers had already employed. For we have seen that the theme had long been current in the French tradition by the time of Ronsard. We have seen too that Petrarchism did not suddenly and inevitably bring about a revolution in France. So much depended on what the individual poet took from the Italian tradition and on how he made use of it. That is why I think the tracing of themes and influences in the context of sixteenth-century French love poetry is such an unrewarding task. The significance of a poet such as Petrarch is far better understood in terms of the example which he set as a writer of serious love poetry than in terms of the themes which he handed down. And the simple truth is that, before the advent of the Pléiade, France produced no poet with both the desire and the talent to follow the example which had been set by the Italian tradition, though it produced many who were content to draw on the common thematic stock. As Marcel Françon puts it: 'ce qu'il y a de nouveau parmi ces poètes de la Pléiade, c'est la volonté déclarée de s'insurger contre le passé',[22] and in any discussion of sixteenth-century French love poetry the significance of this must never be forgotten.

Notes

Introduction

1 The 'Délie' of Maurice Scève, ed. I. D. McFarlane (Cambridge, 1966), p. 29.

2 P. Dronke, Medieval Latin and the Rise of European Love-Lyric, second edition, two vols (Oxford, 1968), p. xvii. See also H.-I. Marrou, 'Au dossier de l'amour courtois', Revue du moyen âge latin, 3 (1947), pp. 81–9.

3 J. Hutton, The Greek Anthology in Italy to the Year 1800 (New York, 1935), p. 46.

4 The Literature of Ancient Egypt, ed. W. K. Simpson (New Haven and London, 1972), pp. 300, 320–1.

5 P. Dronke, The Medieval Lyric (London, 1968), p. 86.

6 'Singing can scarcely be worthwhile, if the song does not come from within the heart; for this reason my song is perfect, for I hold in the joy of love and direct [towards it] my mouth, my eyes, my heart, and my reason.' I use the following edition: Bernard de Ventadour, Chansons d'Amour, ed. Moshé Lazar (Paris, 1966).

7 'In [mutual] harmony and desire is the love of two perfect lovers. No one can have profit [in love] if the desire is not equal. And he is indeed a true fool who criticizes [his lady] for what she desires, and commends to her what is not fitting for her.'

8 'I have indeed well placed my good hope, when she whom most I desire and wish to see shows me a sympathetic face . . .'

9 'The song is perfect and true and good for him who understands it well; and it is [even] better for him who waits for joy. Bernard de Ventadour understands it, composes it and recites it, and hopes for joy from it!'

10 P. Dronke, Medieval Latin, p. 37. On the question of joi and the semantic ramifications of the term, see the numerous examples in A. J. Denomy, 'Jois among the early troubadours: its meaning and possible source', Mediaeval Studies, 13 (1951), pp. 177–217. According to Denomy, Bernard de Ventadour uses the word joi eighty-three times in his poetry.

11 H. Chamard, Les Origines de la poésie française de la Renaissance (Paris, 1920), p. 68.

12 See dizains 376 and 421.

13 Pierre Bec, Manuel pratique de philologie romane, two vols (Paris, 1970–71), I, 126–7.

Chapter 1

1 Strictly speaking, the phrase 'secolo senza poesia' refers to the hundred years following the death of Boccaccio in 1375.

2 D. Poirion, *Le Poète et le prince: l'évolution du lyrisme courtois de Guillaume de Machaut à Charles d'Orléans* (Paris, 1965), p. 255. Marguerite de Navarre, *L'Heptaméron*, ed. M. François (Paris, 1950), pp. 95 and 352, and see n. 274 and 703.

3 *The Literature of Ancient Egypt*, p. 303.

4 Poirion, *op. cit.*, pp. 174–5.

5 *Ibid.*, pp. 189 and 187.

6 Charles d'Orléans, *Poésies*, ed. P. Champion, two vols (Paris, 1923–24), ballade 8.

7 *Le Roman de la Rose*, ed. E. Langlois, five vols (Paris, 1914–24), ll. 2643–53. 'Sweet Thought is the first friend who brings consolation to those caught in the snare of Love, for he reminds them of what Hope has agreed to. When the lover laments and sighs and is in sorrow and torment, Sweet Thought comes from time to time to drive away his wrath and sorrow, and, by his coming, he makes the lover remember that joy which Hope has promised him.'

8 E. R. Curtius, *European Literature and the Latin Middle Ages*, trans. W. R. Trask (New York, 1953), p. 195.

9 L. Forster, *The Icy Fire: Five Studies in European Petrarchism* (Cambridge, 1969), p. 35.

10 'Alas! what is the use of living, if I do not see every day my true and perfect joy in bed, beneath the window, her body white as the snow at Christmas time, so that we can both measure together to see if we are equal [in love]?'

11 D. Page, *Sappho and Alcaeus* (Oxford, 1955); see the discussion of Sappho's poem beginning Φαίνεταί μοι κῆνος ἴσος Θέοισιν, on pp. 19–33.

12 See J. Vianey, *Le Pétrarquisme en France au XVIᵉ siècle* (Paris, 1909); M. Piéri, *Le Pétrarquisme au XVIᵉ siècle...* (Marseille, 1896); V.-L. Saulnier, *Maurice Scève*, two vols (Paris, 1948–49).

13 C. A. Mayer, 'Clément Marot and literary history', in *Studies in French Literature Presented to H. W. Lawton* (Manchester, 1968), pp. 247–60 (p. 255).

14 See Saulnier, *La Littérature française de la Renaissance* (Paris, 1965), p. 65.

15 Mayer, 'Clément Marot and literary history', pp. 255–6.

16 Mayer and D. Bentley-Cranch, 'Clément Marot, poète pétrarquiste', *Bibliothèque d'Humanisme et Renaissance*, 28 (1966), pp. 32–51 (p. 36).

17 Clément Marot, *Œuvres Diverses*, ed. C. A. Mayer (London, 1966),
   No. 26. This edition is hereafter abbreviated *O.D.*

18 'Since you wish to know, my lady, in what state, serving Love, I
   find myself, hear of the wondrous new pain which cruel fate
   constantly causes me. Through the air I go flying, and I am borne
   on tempestuous winds—and [yet] I do not move; and always I feel
   heat and cold together, and I hope [though] abandoned by hope.
   From a mountain clear and covered with white snow issues the
   burning flame which consumes me, and I shiver where my great
   desire sets me on fire. I see Love appearing now grave, now cheer-
   ful; now he runs after me, and now he flees from me: this is my
   death, and this my life.'

19 *Le Jardin de plaisance et fleur de rhétorique*, facsimile reproduction
   of the original edition (published by Antoine Vérard, around
   1501), by the Société des Anciens Textes Français (Paris, 1910),
   fo. cxvi. The last line of the extract quoted is a syllable short:
   presumably one should read something like 'Je suis bien sain . . .'.

20 M. Françon, 'Une Imitation du sonnet de Pétrarque: Pace non
   trovo . . .', *Italica*, 20 (1943), pp. 127–31 (p. 131).

21 Mayer and Bentley-Cranch, 'Clément Marot, poète pétrarquiste',
   p. 41. M. White, 'Petrarchism in the French Rondeau before 1527',
   French Studies, 22 (1968), pp. 287–95 (p. 290). Maurice Scève,
   Délie, ed. E. Parturier (Paris, 1916), p. xiv.

22 Marot, *O.D.*, No. 25, note 1.

23 In *Documents inédits sur l'histoire de France: Recueil d'Arts de
   Seconde Rhétorique*, ed. E. Langlois (Paris, 1902), p. 182.

24 Pietro Bembo, *Prose e rime*, ed. C. Dionisotti, second edition
   (Turin, 1966), pp. 397–8. These lines form the final stanza of a
   canzone beginning 'Preso al primo apparir del vostro raggio'
   which appears in bk. 2 of the *Asolani*. The poet describes how his
   heart has left him and gone to dwell with the heart of his beloved,
   and then he concludes: 'But, as if moved by a noble desire not to
   share its kingdom with another, or as if heaven had directed it
   [i.e. the heart of his beloved] towards that place where no other
   lord was ever to go, there, whence my heart had departed, yours
   came joyfully. Thus they exchanged abodes, and from that time
   onwards your heart dwells with me and mine with yours.'

25 See, on the conceit of the exchange of hearts, Mayer and
   Bentley-Cranch, 'Le Premier Pétrarquiste français, Jean Marot',
   Bibliothèque d'Humanisme et Renaissance, 27 (1965), pp. 183–5
   (p. 185, n. 2). The passage from Robert Breton is quoted in C.
   Ruutz-Rees, *Charles de Sainte-Marthe* (New York, 1910), p. 605.

26 C. Ruutz-Rees, *op. cit.*, p. 334.

27 P. M. Smith, *Clément Marot* (London, 1970), p. 141.

28 White, *op. cit.*, p. 290. She gives the full text of the Picart poem.

For an interesting example of the ice and fire antithesis in antiquity, see 'Longinus', *On the Sublime*, ed. D. A. Russell (Oxford, 1964), 10:3.

29 Charles d'Orléans, *op. cit.*, ballade 100.
30 Charles d'Orléans, *op. cit.*, ballade 123ᵉ.
31 In *Documents inédits sur l'histoire de France*, p. liii.
32 Marot, *O.D.*, No. 55, n. 2.
33 See *Documents inédits sur l'histoire de France*, p. 353, n. 1.
34 E. M. Rutson, 'A note on Jean Marot's debt to Italian sources', *Modern Language Review*, 61 (1966), pp. 25–8. White, *op. cit.*, p. 288.
35 Quoted, with the Italian text of Serafino, in Mayer and Bentley-Cranch, 'Le Premier Pétrarquiste français, Jean Marot'.
36 C. S. Lewis, *English Literature in the Sixteenth Century* (Oxford, 1954), p. 223.
37 Charles d'Orléans, *op. cit.*, rondeau 1.
38 L. Forster, *op. cit.*, pp. 82–3.
39 H. Weber, *La Création poétique au XVIᵉ siècle en France*, two vols (Paris, 1956), p. 162.
40 Maurice Scève, *Délie*, ed. E. Parturier, p. xxii.
41 G. Tracconaglia, *Une Page de l'histoire de l'italianisme à Lyon...* (Lodi, 1915–17), p. 11.
42 White, *op. cit.*, p. 294.
43 Lewis, *op. cit.*, p. 55.
44 Saulnier, *Maurice Scève*, pp. 208–9.

Chapter 2

1 Saulnier, *Maurice Scève*, p. 562.
2 G. Poulet, *Mesure de l'instant* (Paris, 1968), p. 25.
3 See, for example, L. Goldman, 'Samuel Daniel's *Delia* and the emblem tradition', *Journal of English and Germanic Philology*, 67 (1968), pp. 49–63.
4 D. G. Coleman, 'Scève's choice of the name "Délie"', *French Studies*, 18 (1964), pp. 1–16. E. Giudici, *Maurice Scève: poeta della Délie*, two vols (Rome, 1965–68), I, 129.
5 In *Maurice Scève: Opere poetiche minori*, ed. E. Giudici (Naples, 1965), p. 255.
6 See H. Redman, jr, 'A proposed identification for Maurice Scève's Délie', *Renaissance News*, 10 (1957), pp. 188–93. Redman's identification of Délie with Anne de Pisseleu, whose family name was d'Heilly, has not been generally accepted, however.
7 'Like Hecate you will make me wander / Alive and dead a hundred years among the Shades. / Like Diana in the Heavens you will have me confined, / From which you descended to these

mortal miseries. / As one reigning in the infernal shadows / You
will lessen or increase my sufferings. / But as the Moon, flowing
in my veins, / Such you were, are, and will be, Délie, / The one
that Cupid has joined to my vain thoughts / So strongly that
Death will never release it from them.' All translations from the
Délie are taken with kind permission, from the unpublished
doctoral thesis by R. A. Hallett: 'A Translation, with introduction
and notes, of the *Délie* of Maurice Scève', The Pennsylvania
State University, 1973.

8 F. Desonay, *Ronsard, poète de l'amour*, three vols (Brussels, 1952–9),
I, 78–9.

9 Weber, *op. cit.*, p. 226.

10 Quoted in Parturier's edition of the *Délie*, p. xxxi.

11 *L'Art Poëtique de Jacques Peletier du Mans (1555)*, ed. A. Boulanger
(Paris, 1930), p. 77.

12 P. Boutang, *Commentaire sur quarante-neuf dizains de la Délie* (Paris,
1953), pp. 82–4. Weber follows Boutang's reading in his *La
Création poétique . . .*, pp. 198–9.

13 See the interesting ramifications of the word *ruin* in English, discussed in O. Barfield, *Poetic Diction* (London, 1952), chapter VII.

14 R. A. Hallett's tanslation of the complete poem reads as follows:
'See the bright day spoil into darkness, / Whereas its light preserves its benefit; / Joyous deeds end with a dirge / Though
pleasure do its utmost against trouble. / All greatness is abruptly
brought down, / So feeble is the giver of our pleasures. / And
though the trees grow tall and green with leaves, their honor, /
Insignificant glory, finally falls to earth, / Whereas your lofty good
alone will have the fortune / To remain eternally verdant on your
famous tomb.'

15 For Petrarch's comments on the significance of the laurel, see
'Petrarch's coronation oration' [trans. by E. H. Wilkins], *Publications of the Modern Language Association of America*, 68 (1953), pp.
1241–50.

16 H. Jacoubet, *Jean de Boyssonné et son temps* (Toulouse and Paris,
1930), p. 107. Giudici, I, 32.

17 M. Françon, 'Sur les allusions historiques de la "Délie" de Maurice
Scève', *Le lingue straniere*, 14 (1965), pp. 26–8. Françon, 'Studies
on Maurice Scève's *Délie*', *Romance Notes*, 6 (1964–65), pp. 160–7.

18 Several critics have attempted to relate all the historical dizains to
the central love experience of the *Délie*, but I do not find their
efforts convincing. See D. L. Cook, 'The political *Dizains* of the
Délie', *Bibliothèque d'Humanisme et Renaissance*, 29 (1967), pp.
339–55. R. Mulhauser, 'The historic allusion poems in the *Délie*
of Maurice Scève', *Symposium*, 16 (1962), pp. 136–43.

19 'To aspire always to that which is outside one's power / To

obtain, and to always persist / Without taking up reason's neces-
sities, / Against which one cannot resist, / Would it not be to
encourage danger / And to fabricate one's downfall? / Would it
not be, without expectation / Of any profit, to put honor at its
mercy, / Or to risk one's reputation / For much less than Charles
for Landrecies?'

20 R. Mulhauser, *op. cit.*, p. 142.

21 'And the fruit of my having strayed from the right was is shame
and repentance, and the clear recognition that whatever is pleasing
in this world is a brief dream.' (Or, 'whatever the world loves').

22 L. Harvey, *The Aesthetics of the Renaissance Love Sonnet*(Geneva,
1962), p. 84.

23 D. Stone, jr, *Ronsard's Sonnet Cycles* (New Haven and London,
1966), p. 192.

24 G. Saba, *La poesia di Joachim du Bellay* (Messina and Florence, 1962),
p. 65.

25 Lewis, *op cit.*, p. 327.

26 A.-M. Schmidt, *Études sur le XVIe siècle* (Paris, 1967), p. 134, n. 1.

27 R. D. Cottrell, 'Pernette du Guillet's *Rymes*: an adventure in ideal
love', *Bibliothèque d'Humanisme et Renaissance*, 31 (1969), pp. 553–71
(p. 553). McFarlane's comments may be found in his edition of the
Délie, p. 91.

28 'A so holy flame will remain, in its brightness, / Always shining,
for all to see, / As long as this World will last / And Love wil be
held in reverence. / And so I see little difference / Between this
ardor which will pursue our hearts / And the living virtue which
will follow us / Beyond the amply long and wide Heavens. / Thus
will our Juniper live, / Uninjured by any mortal Oblivion.'

29 Compare Giudici's interpretation of this poem in his *Maurice
Scève: poeta della Délie*, II, 740–1.

30 Text and an interesting discussion in J. Horrent, 'Défense et illustration de *L'Olive*', *Cahiers d'analyse textuelle*, 10 (1968), pp.
93–116. 'There is that highest good which every man desires; there
the true repose; there the peace which in vain you seek constantly
in this world.'

31 É. Faguet, *Seizième siècle: Études littéraires* (Paris, 1894), p. 241.

32 A. Glauser, *Le Poème-Symbole* (Paris, 1967), p. 34.

33 G. Santayana, *Interpretations of Poetry and Religion* (New York,
1924), p. 120.

34 Text in *Poeti del duecento*, edited by G. Contini, two vols (Milan
and Naples, 1960), II, 522–9. 'From its power [i.e. the power of
love], death often results, if by chance that virtue [i.e. reason]
which supports the opposite way [i.e. the way of life rather than
death] should be impeded. Not because it [love] is opposed to
nature (does it cause death), but inasmuch as a man is turned by

fate away from the perfect good, he cannot claim to be alive, since he has no firm control over himself.' These are ll. 35–41 of the canzone. See also the notes in *Poeti del dolce stil nuovo*, ed. M. Marti (Florence, 1969), pp. 183–91; and the book by J. E. Shaw, *Guido Cavalcanti's Theory of Love: The Canzone d'Amore and other Related Problems* (Toronto, 1949).

35 Saulnier, *Maurice Scève*, pp. 244–5.

36 Weber, *Le Langage poétique de Maurice Scève dans la 'Délie'* (Florence, 1948), p. 36.

37 Saulnier, *Maurice Scève*, p. 157.

38 Pernette du Guillet, *Rymes*, ed. V. E. Graham (Geneva, 1968), p. 22.

39 Saulnier, 'Étude sur Pernette du Guillet et ses *Rymes*', *Bibliothèque d'Humanisme et Renaissance*, 4 (1944), pp. 7–119 (p. 100). See H. Staub, *Le Curieux désir: Scève et Peletier du Mans, poètes de la connaissance* (Geneva, 1967), p. 44.

40 'My languishing multiplies the pain / Of the strong desire whose hope you hold. / My firm loving makes you sure and certain of it / By means of my long suffering, which gave that assurance. / But you being proud of my suffering, / And taking it for your amusement, / You keep me in this state of contentment / (Although it is vain) by hope, which attracts me, / Since we both live from a kind of nourishment, / Me from loving you, and you from my martyrdom.'

41 Chamard, *op. cit.*, p. 73.

42 Saulnier, 'Étude sur Pernette', pp. 87–8.

43 Lewis, *op. cit.*, p. 224.

44 Weber, *La Création poétique*, p. 226.

45 'To a lofty good of such holy friendship / You ought easily to be incited, / If not by duty or honest pity, / At least by my loyal persistance, / In order to sit, united and together / In peace above on our eternal throne. / Do you not see the Rhône from the West, / Turn and flow towards the South, / Just to flow together with its Saône / All the way to their Sea where both will die?'

46 'The day, now gone, of your sweet presence / Was a day cloudless and bright in a dark winter, / A day which makes the night of your absence, / To my mind's eye, a far blacker time / Than is, to my Body, this enervating existence / Which now denies itself to me. / For, as soon as you were gone, / Like the Hare crouched in its burrow, / I intently listen, hearing a muffled noise, / Quite astray in the Egyptian darkness.'

47 'See how with Winter trembling in its place of sojourn / The trees are faded in their bare fields. / Then, when Springtime brings back the beautiful weather, / They have buds, leaves, flowers, fruit springing forth. / Trees, bushes, hedges and copse / Bedeck them-

selves then in their gay verdure. / As long as your ungrateful coldness hangs on me / My hope is stripped of its green growth. / Then, with the sweet Spring returning, without coldness, / My life blossoms forth into its superb April.'

48 Saulnier, *Maurice Scève*, p. 142.

49 'Moisture, my eyes' Water-clock, / Is caused to flow always in a circular manner by my pitiless one, / Following my sighs, / Which attract it there in place of air from the empty places. / Thus the moisture at all times descends, mounts and does the same again, / To flood and quench my flames. / Is it then so easy for me to weep / These tears that they should fall without cease? / Alas, from the highest point they flow, drop by drop, / Falling upon the breast from which they are drawn.' I would amend to 'breasts' in the final line.

Chapter 3

1 Saulnier, 'Étude sur Pernette', pp. 56–7. Saulnier, *Maurice Scève*, p. 206.

2 J. B. Wadsworth, *Lyons 1473–1503: The Beginnings of Cosmopolitanism* (Cambridge, Massachusetts, 1962), p. x.

3 S. M. Stern, 'Esistono dei rapporti letterari tra il mondo islamico e l'Europa occidentale nell' alto medio evo?', in *L'Occidente e l'Islam nell' alto medioevo*, conference proceedings published by the Centro italiano di studi sull' alto medioevo, two vols (Spoleto, 1965), p. 655.

4 *Anthologia Palatina* 5.155. I have taken the text from the following edition: *The Greek Anthology: Hellenistic Epigrams*, ed. A. S. F. Gow and D. L. Page, two vols (Cambridge, 1965), I, 229. 'Within my heart Eros himself has formed the sweetly-speaking Heliodora, the soul of my soul.'

5 Serafino Aquilano, *Opere* (Venice, 1548), fo. 125 and fo. 143 v. See the poems beginning 'Se drento porto una fornace ardente . . .' and 'Che non se placa hormai tua cruda mente'. I have used British Library copy 11429. df. 35. I have also used the edition of Serafino's strambotti by Barbara Bauer-Formiconi (Munich, 1967), and have occasionally modified my quotations from the 1548 edition as a result.

6 Text in H.-J. Molinier, *Mellin de Saint-Gelays* (Rodez, 1910), p. 560.

7 H. Hauvette, *Les Poésies lyriques de Pétrarque* (Paris, 1931), p. 142.

8 Desonay, *op. cit.*, I, 35–6.

9 Saulnier, *Maurice Scève*, p. 270. Desonay, *op. cit.*, I, 93, and see also pp. 79, 115, 120, etc.

10 I. Murray, 'Oscar Wilde's absorption of "influences": the case

history of Chuang Tzu', *Durham University Journal*, 64 (1971–72), [new series, vol. 33], pp. 1–13 (p. 1).

11 J. Aynard, *Les Poètes lyonnais précurseurs de la Pléiade* (Paris, 1924), p. 13.

12 Saulnier, *Maurice Scève*, pp. 205 and 142.

13 Vianey, *op. cit.*, p. 7.

14 Saulnier, *Maurice Scève*, p. 208.

15 C. Pellegrini, 'Il Petrarca nella cultura francese', in *Tradizione italiana e cultura europea* (Messina, 1947), pp. 5–18.

16 Jean Lemaire de Belges, *Œuvres*, ed. J. Stecher, four vols (Louvain, 1882–85), III, 102.

17 From an early version of the 'Temple de Cupido' in *L'Adolescence Clémentine*, ed. Saulnier (Paris, 1958), p. 245.

18 In the *De la louenge et excellence des bons facteurs qui bien ont composé en rime, tant deça que delà les monts*, quoted by W. F. Patterson, *Three Centuries of French Poetic Theory*, two vols (Ann Arbor, Michigan, 1935), pp. 163–4.

19 E. H. Wilkins, *Studies in the Life and Works of Petrarch* (Cambridge, Massachusetts, 1955), p. 289.

20 See du Bellay, first preface to the *Olive*.

21 Peletier du Mans, *Art Poëtique*, ed. A. Boulanger, p. 165. Peletier speaks of Petrarch in the following rather curious terms: 'Nous l'avons tous admiré, e imité: non sans cause: vù la grand' dousseur du stile, la grand' variete sus un seul Suget . . . Combien qu'il à des redites: e que quelquefoes il conclue un peu froedemant. Mes il n'ctoct pas né du bon tans.'

22 Claude Fauchet, *Recueil de l'origine de la langue et poésie française, rime et romans*, reprint of the 1581 Paris edition (Geneva, 1972), p. 47.

23 Henri Estienne, *Project du livre intitulé: De la precellence du langage françois*, reprint of the 1579 Paris edition (Geneva, 1972), preface. Later in the book Estienne quotes a canzone by Bembo, with a French translation by Philippe Desportes (1546–1606), pp. 62–3. The last stanza of this canzone I quoted earlier in connection with the poetry of Marot (see above p. 28), and readers may wish to compare the relevant texts.

24 Fauchet, *op. cit.*, p. 49.

25 *Chansons de Gace Brulé*, ed. G. Huet (Paris, 1902), p. 19.

26 *Œuvres de Guillaume de Machaut*, ed. E. Hœpffner, three vols (Paris, 1908–21), III. The line is from *La Fonteinne amoureuse* (l. 331).

27 See the second volume of the edition of the *Jardin* published by the Société des Anciens Textes Français (p. 23).

28 C. Ruutz-Rees, *op cit.*, pp. 269–70.

29 Françon, 'Une Imitation du sonnet de Pétrarque . . .', p. 130.

30 Text in *Maurice Scève: Opere poetiche minori*, ed. Giudici, p. 206. (The *Petit Oeuvre d'amour* has been attributed to Scève: see McFarlane's edition of the *Délie*, p. 10, for further reference.)

31 'I cannot find peace, and I haven't the wherewithal to make war; and I fear and hope, and burn and I am [like] ice, and I fly above the sky and lie on the ground, and I can grasp nothing and [yet] all the world I embrace . . .'

32 A. H. Schutz, *Vernacular Books in Parisian Private Libraries of the Sixteenth Century according to the Notarial Inventories* (Chapel Hill, North Carolina, 1955), p. 23.

33 In *Chanson & Madrigal, 1480–1530*, ed. J. Haar (Cambridge, Massachusetts, 1964), pp. 118–19.

34 Vianey, *op. cit.*, pp. 51 ff.

35 Text in Pernette du Guillet, *Rymes*, ed. V. Graham, pp. 152–3. See J. G. Fucilla, 'Sources of du Bellay's *Contre les Pétrarquistes*', *Modern Philology*, 28 (1930–31), pp. 1–11.

36 Forster, *op. cit.*, p. 9.

37 J. Moderne, *Le Parangon des chansons* (Lyon, 1538–41), bk. 1, fo. 6. I have used British Library copy K. 10. a. 9.

38 Mellin de Saint-Gelais, *Œuvres complètes*, ed. P. Blanchemain, three vols (Paris, 1873), II, 85.

39 Weber, *Le Langage poétique de Maurice Scève*, p. 20.

40 'This beauty, which embellished the world / When she in whom I live dying was born, / Has imprinted in my eyes / Not only her living features, / But so keeps my faculties stunned / With admiration of her admirable marvels . . .'

41 'This link of gold [i.e. a strand of Délie's hair], ray from you my Sun, / Who with your arm enslave my Soul and life, / So strongly holds my gaze / That it has completely drawn my thought to you, / Demonstrating to me surely that it is worthwhile / For me to put myself under your tutelage.'

42 See A. Cartier, *Bibliographie des éditions des de Tournes, imprimeurs lyonnais*, two vols (Paris, 1937–8), I, 199, 225.

43 G. Dottin, 'Aspects littéraires de la chanson "musicale" à l'époque de Marot', *Revue des Sciences Humaines* (1964), pp. 425–32 (pp. 426–7).

44 F. Lesure, *Musicians and Poets of the French Renaissance*, trans. E. Gianturco and H. Rosenwald (New York, 1955), pp. 80–1.

45 D. Heartz, in *Chanson & Madrigal*, ed. J. Haar, pp. 96–7.

46 M. Dassonville, 'Maurice Scève, poète lyonnais', *L'Espirit créateur*, 5 (1965), pp. 71–9 (p. 73).

47 Both these Italian passages are quoted in É. Picot, *Les Français italianisants au XVIe siècle*, two vols (Paris, 1906–7), I, 167, 156–7.

48 See *Le rime di Serafino de' Ciminelli dall' Aquila*, ed. M. Menghini (Bologna, 1894), p. 14.

49 *Le rime di Serafino*, ed. M. Menghini, pp. 1–2 and 4.

50 See Mayer and Bentley-Cranch, 'Clément Marot, poète pétrarquiste', p. 44.

51 *Ibid.*

52 Weber, *La Création poétique*, p. 232.

53 Serafino, *Opere*, fo. 102 v.

54 Saulnier, *Maurice Scève*, p. 265.

55 'Traitorous, secret suffering, so you assail me, / As though your victory were complete, / Distilling from evil's Alembic / The very breath and pulse of my life.'

56 Serafino, *Opere*, fo. 107 v. These lines are from the *Disperata prima*. 'Then let death loosen and tighten the chain in a moment, and tear me to pieces; so may I lose my voice, my heartbeats, and my breath.'

57 Serafino, *Opere*, fo. 157 v. 'The sailor puts up with fortune and the winds only in order to reach his desired haven; the good soldier never pays regard to hardship, for he waits for booty as his consolation.'

58 Serafino, *Opere*, fo. 126 v. The reference is incorrectly given in the Parturier and McFarlane editions of the *Délie*. 'When from the high mountains the shadow descends, and the stars drive out the clear day, every tired animal rests in the shadow, and the labours of the day are forgotten. Alas! I languish and weep . . .'

59 From the *Eglogue de Marot au Roy, soubz les noms de Pan & Robin*, ll. 61–2, in Clément Marot, *Œuvres Lyriques*, ed. C. A. Mayer (London, 1964), No. 89 (Eglogue III).

60 'When Dawn comes to render apparent to us / What the darkness of the gloom hides, / The night fire in my transparent body / Returns to my heart which covers many sparks, / And when Vesper comes to spread / His shady veil on universal earth, / My flame leaves its dismal pit / Where is the abyss so harmful to my bright day, / And illumines again the shady night, / Attending the shining glow-worm.'

61 Serafino, *Opere*, fo. 153. 'I go unseen over slopes and fields, for the smoke of my burning passion keeps me hidden; and if, sometimes, the flames escape from my breast, they make me appear like a firefly in August.' It will be obvious that there is not much connection between the Serafino text and dizain 355 of the *Délie*. Parturier, who first suggested the connection was probably confused by the Italian *lucciola* (= 'firefly', as in Dante, *Inferno*, XXVI, l. 29, where it is used in a long simile based on the light of the firefly in summer) and *lucciolo* (= 'glow-worm').

62 B. G. Chariteo, *Le rime*, ed. E. Pèrcopo, two vols (Naples, 1892), sonnet 20.

63 *Ibid.*, sonnet 37.

64 'If ever Death was sweetly dear, / To my sweet soul now is it
dearly pleasing . . . Wherefore, as in the fire the feathered Phoenix,
/ This hope [the 'esperance' of l. 8] dies and is reborn in me a
hundred times a day.' For Sannazaro's lines, see McFarlane's
edition of the *Délie*, p. 385, and see also the notes to dizains 167 and
288.

65 Bembo, *Prose e rime*, p. 546 (from the sonnet beginning 'Solingo
augello, se piangendo vai').

66 L. Martelli, *Le rime volgari* (Rome, 1533), fo. ci v.

67 Weber, *Le Langage poétique de Maurice Scève*, pp. 43–4.

68 L. Ariosto, *Orlando furioso*, ed. L. Caretti (Milan and Naples, 1954),
canto 11, stanza 65. 'Her lovely face was as sometimes the sky in
spring is wont to be, when the rain is falling and at the same time
the sun breaks through the misty veil which surrounds it. And
as the nightingale then sings sweet songs among the green branches
of the tree, so Love bathes his wings in her beautiful tears, and
rejoices in the limpid light.'

69 See Picot, *Les Italiens en France au XVIe siècle* (Bordeaux, 1901–2),
pp. 112–13.

70 D. G. Coleman, *Maurice Scève: Poet of Love* (Cambridge, 1975),
and 'Some notes on Scève and Petrarch'. *French Studies*, 14 (1960),
pp. 293–303. D. Fenoaltea, 'Patterns of poetry in the *Délie*'
(unpublished doctoral dissertation, Harvard University, 1971), and
'The poet in nature: sources of Scève's *Délie* in Petrarch's *Rime*',
French Studies, 27 (1973), pp. 257–70.

71 F. Petrarca, *Rime, Trionfi e poesie latine*, ed. F. Neri and others
(Milan and Naples, 1951), p. 500. The line is from the *Triumphus
Cupidinis*, III, 168.

72 'You who hear in scattered rhymes the sound of those sighs with
which I used to nourish my heart in [the time of] my first youthful
error, when I was in part another man than the one I am now . . .'
Petrarch fell in love with Laura at the age of twenty-three, on
6 April 1327. R. A. Hallett translates the opening lines of the *Délie*
as follows: 'My Eye, too ardent in my youthful gallivanting, / Was
turning round about, imprudent, without purpose . . .'

73 D. G. Coleman, *Maurice Scève*, p. 24.

74 'Perhaps in vain I scatter my words, but I declare to you that you
are suffering from a terrible and deadly lethargy' (*Triumphus
Temporis*, ll. 73–5).

75 'I seek out the most solitary places / Where despair and horror live
/ To make them the confidants of my ills, / Ills devoid, most surely,
of any good, / Which, accustomed to harm others as well as me,
/ Still cause fear, even in solitude. / Since I feel that my life is in
such disequilibrium / That the more I flee both night and day / Her
beautiful holy eyes, the farther I am from servitude / In my

thought, these solitary places are a sweet sojourn.'
76 'Through the middle of the wild and inhospitable woods, where armed men go at great risk, I go without fear. For no one can make me frightened, except that Sun whose rays are those of living Love. And I go singing, o my foolish thoughts, her whom not even heaven could make distant from me, since I have her in my eyes; and it seems to me I see women and girls with her, and they are firs and beech-trees. It seems I hear her, hearing the branches and the breezes and the leaves and the birds lamenting, and the murmuring waters swiftly flowing through the green grass. Rarely did ever silence or the solitary terror of a shady wood please me so much; except that it is too far from my Sun.' (Or, 'except that too much of my Sun is lost'.)
77 Santayana, *op. cit.*, p. 130.
78 See L. A. Magnery, 'Valéry et Pétrarque à la lumière d'un texte peu connu', *Studi francesi*, 44 (1971), pp. 254–61.
79 Quoted in G. Spagnoletti, *Il Petrarchismo* (Milan, 1959), p. 112. 'Never will he seem to me a poet who with his song nourishes only my ear.'
80 Schutz, *op. cit.*, p. 25 and p. 20.
81 Saulnier, *Maurice Scève*, p. 279.
82 Dottin, *op. cit.*, p. 428. The text of the Chartier poem ('Triste plaisir et doloreuse joye') may be found in *The Poetical Works of Alain Chartier*, ed. J. C. Laidlaw (Cambridge, 1974); or, with music by Binchois, in E. Droz and G. Thibault, *Poètes et musiciens du XVᵉ siècle* (Paris, 1924).
83 *I dialogi di Messer Speron Sperone* (Venice, 1542), fo. 19.
84 *I dialogi*, fo. 14. See A. Béguin, *Poésie de la présence* (Neuchâtel, 1957), p. 89. The image is already in Petrarch's sestina beginning 'A qualunque animale alberga in terra', ll. 13–14.
85 *I dialogi*, fo. 14 v.
86 For full details, see the editions of the *Délie* by McFarlane or Parturier.
87 *I dialogi*, fo. 21.
88 Françon, 'Pétrarque et Cément Marot', *Italica*, 40 (1963), pp. 18–21 (p. 20).

Chapter 4

1 *Poésies complètes du troubadour Marcabru*, ed. J.-M.-L. Dejeanne (Toulouse, 1909), No. 14, 'My desire and its outward manifestation are, and are not, of the same form, since from the desire is born its manifestation and since [at the same time] she [the lady] forms it with her words. For if the one [desire] leads the fool into the trap, the other [its manifestation? or her words?] keeps him

stuck fast.' For other interpretations, see L. M. Paterson, *Troubadours and Eloquence* (Oxford, 1975), pp. 44–5.

2 C. Muscatine, 'The emergence of psychological allegory in Old French Romance', *Publications of the Modern Language Association of Amercia*, 68 (1953), pp. 1160–82.

3 Weber, *Le Language poétique de Maurice Scève*, p. 45.

4 Saulnier, *Maurice Scève*, p. 284.

5 W. Empson, *The Structure of Complex Words* (London, 1951), p. 346.

6 Saulnier, *Maurice Scève*, p. 284.

7 A. D. Scaglione, *Nature and Love in the Late Middle Ages* (Berkeley, California, 1963), p. 36.

8 P. Zumthor, 'Charles d'Orléans et le langage de l'allégorie', in *Mélanges offerts à Rita Lejeune*, two vols (Gembloux, 1969), pp. 1481–502 (p. 1501).

9 J. Fox, *The Lyric Poetry of Charles d'Orléans* (Oxford, 1969), p. 75.

10 Empson, *op. cit.*, p. 347.

11 Quoted in Fox, *op. cit.*, p. 75, note 1.

12 Fox, *op. cit.*, pp. 56 and 69–70.

13 D. G. Coleman, 'Images in Scève's "Délie" ', *Modern Language Review*, 59 (1964), pp. 375–86.

14 D. G. Coleman, 'The emblesmes and images in Maurice Scève's "Délie" ' (unpublished doctoral dissertation, Glasgow University, 1962), p. 138.

15 H. Vernay, *Les Divers Sens du mot 'Raison' autour de l'œuvre de Marguerite d'Angoulême, reine de Navarre (1492–1549)* (Heidelberg, 1962), p. 153.

16 B. G. Chariteo, *Le rime*, sonnets 81 and 50.

17 Saulnier, *Maurice Scève*, p. 237.

18 *Ibid.*, See also vol. II, p. 109, n. 118.

19 Weber, 'Y a-t-il une poésie hermétique au XVIᵉ siècle en France?', *Cahiers de l'Association Internationale des Études Françaises*, 15 (1963), pp. 41–58 (p. 54).

20 *Jardin*, folios lxxi v., lxii.

21 Saulnier, *Maurice Scève*, p. 238. Vernay, *op. cit.*, p. 87.

22 Saulnier, *Maurice Scève*, p. 237. See also vol. II, pp. 109–10, n. 120.

23 F. Simone, *Il rinascimento francese* (Turin, 1961), p. 207.

24 Marot, O.D., No. 43. Scève uses the same rhyme in dizain 401 of the *Délie*.

25 Ronsard, *Les Amours*, ed. H. Weber and C. Weber (Paris, 1963), p. 266. This poem is No. 12 in the *Second Livre des Meslanges (1559)*. All quotations from the poetry of Ronsard are taken from the Weber edition, unless otherwise specified.

Chapter 5

1 J. Tortel, *Poésies de Maurice Scève* (Lausanne, 1961), p. 14.

2 The verb *pétrarquiser* is apparently first used by du Bellay, in 1550.

3 This looks forward to the composition of the *Franciade*, Ronsard's epic poem, which finally appeared, though in an unfinished state, in 1572.

4 A. Héroët, *Œuvres poétiques*, ed. F. Gohin (Paris, 1909), p. 70.

5 Desonay, *op. cit.*, I, 78.

6 Giudici, *Maurice Scève: poeta della Délie*, I, 160.

7 Weber, *Le Langage poétique de Maurice Scève*, p. 54. See also W. v. Wartburg, *Évolution et structure de la langue française*, seventh edition (Bern, 1965), p. 157.

8 J. Molinet, *Les Faictz et ditz*, ed. N. Dupire, three vols (Paris, 1936–39), III, 572.

9 F. De Sanctis, *Saggio critico sul Petrarca* (Bari, 1954), p. 75. Chamard, *Joachim du Bellay* (Lille, 1900), p 179.

10 J. H. Whitfield, *A Short History of Italian Literature* (Harmondsworth, 1960), p. 28.

11 A. Gendre, *Ronsard, poète de la conquête amoreuse* (Neuchâtel, 1970), p. 49.

12 See du Bellay, *La Deffence et illustration de la langue françoyse*, ed. H. Chamard (Paris, 1948), p. 108.

13 See Giudici, *Maurice Scève: poeta della Délie*, I, 164–5.

14 Saint-Gelais, *op. cit.*, II, 85.

15 Weber, *La Création poétique*, p. 291.

16 Shakespeare, *The Sonnets*, ed. J. Dover Wilson, second edition (Cambridge, 1967), No. 33.

17 Curtius, *op. cit.*, pp. 183 and 92–3.

18 E. de Beaulieu, *Les Divers Rapportz*, edited by M. A. Pegg (Geneva, 1964), p. 167.

19 G. Castor, *Pléiade Poetics* (Cambridge, 1964), p. 55.

20 The two volumes of this anthology first appeared in 1545 and 1547.

21 R. Lebègue, 'Un Volume de vers italiens annotés par Ronsard', *Bulletin du bibliophile* (1951), pp. 273–80 (p. 278). Ronsard's annotations were made around 1551.

22 Françon, 'Pétrarque et Clément Marot', p. 20.

Select bibliography

Editions of the *Délie* of Maurice Scève

Délie: Object de plus haulte vertu, ed. E. Parturier (Paris, 1916). All quotations from the *Délie* in this book are taken from Parturier's edition.

The 'Délie' of Maurice Scève, ed. I. D. McFarlane (Cambridge, 1966).

The English translations from the *Délie* which appear in this book are taken from the following work:

R. A. Hallett, 'A translation, with introduction and notes, of the *Délie* of Maurice Scève' (unpublished doctoral dissertation, The Pennsylvania State University, 1973).

Editions of the collected works of Scève

Œuvres poétiques complètes de Maurice Scève . . ., ed. B. Guégan (Paris, 1927).

Maurice Scève: Œuvres complètes, ed. P. Quignard (Paris, 1974).

Critical studies on Scève

J. -P. Attal, 'Etat présent des études scéviennes', *Critique*, 16 (1960), pp. 3–23.

A. Baur, *Maurice Scève et la Renaissance lyonnaise* (Paris, 1906).

D. R. Bienaimé, 'I più recenti sviluppi degli studi su Maurice Scève (1949–1966)', *Studi francesi*, 12 (1968), pp. 1–8.

P. Boutang, *Commentaire sur quarante-neuf dizains de la Délie* (Paris, 1953).

D. G. Coleman, 'Some notes on Scève and Petrarch', *French Studies*, 14 (1960), pp. 293–303.

—— 'Images in Scève's "Délie" ', *Modern Language Review*, 59 (1964), pp. 375–86.

—— 'Scève's choice of the name "Délie" ', *French Studies*, 18 (1964), pp. 1–16.

—— 'Propertius, Petrarch and Scève', *Kentucky Romance Quarterly*, 18 (1971), pp. 77–89.

—— *Maurice Scève: Poet of Love—Tradition and Originality* (Cambridge, 1975).

D. Fenoaltea, 'The Poet in nature: sources of Scève's *Délie* in Petrarch's *Rime*', *French Studies*, 27 (1973), pp. 257–70.

E. Giudici, *Maurice Scève: poeta della Délie*, two vols (Rome, 1965–68).

I. D. McFarlane, 'Notes on Maurice Scève's *Délie*', *French Studies*, 13 (1959), pp. 99–111.

V. -L. Saulnier, *Maurice Scève*, two vols (Paris 1948–49).

H. Staub, *Le Curieux Désir: Scève et Peletier du Mans, poètes de la connaissance* (Geneva, 1967).

H. Weber, *Le Langage poétique de Maurice Scève dans la 'Délie'* (Florence, 1948).

——— *La Création poétique au XVIe siècle en France* . . ., 2 vols (Paris, 1956), pp. 161–230 ('La poésie amoureuse de Maurice Scève').

D. B. Wilson, 'Remarks on Maurice Scève's *Délie*', *Durham University Journal*, 60 (1967–68), [new series, vol. 29], pp. 7–12.

Italian literature and the Petrarchan background

(a) Texts

L. Ariosto, *Orlando furioso*, ed. L. Caretti (Milan and Naples, 1954).

P. Bembo, *Prose e rime*, ed. C. Dionisotti, second edition (Turin, 1966).

B. G. Chariteo, *Le rime*, ed. E. Pèrcopo, two vols (Naples, 1892).

F. Petrarca, *Rime, Trionfi e poesie latine*, ed. F. Neri and others (Milan and Naples, 1951). All quotations from Petrarch are taken from this edition.

Le rime di Serafino de' Ciminelli dall' Aquila, ed. M. Menghini (Bologna, 1894).

Die Strambotti des Serafino dall' Aquila . . ., ed. B. Bauer-Formiconi (Munich, 1967).

I dialogi di Messer Speron Sperone (Venice, 1542). I have used British Library Copy 714. a. 16.

(b) Critical studies

E. Caldarini, 'Nuove fonti italiane dell' *Olive*', *Bibliothèque d'Humanisme et Renaissance*, 27 (1965), pp. 395–434.

R. J. Clements, 'Anti-Petrarchism of the Pléiade', *Modern Philology*, 39 (1941–42), pp. 15–21.

L. Forster, *The Icy Fire: Five Studies in European Petrarchism* (Cambridge, 1969).

M. Françon, 'Sur l'influence de Pétrarque en France aux XVe et XVIe siècles', *Italica*, 19 (1942), pp. 105–10.

——— 'Une Imitation du sonnet de Pétrarque: Pace non trovo . . .', *Italica*, 20 (1943), pp. 127–31.

—— 'Vasquin Philieul, traducteur de Pétrarque', *French Studies*, 4 (1950), pp. 216–26.

—— 'Pétrarque et Clément Marot', *Italica*, 40 (1963), pp. 18–21.

J. G. Fucilla, 'Sources of du Bellay's *Contre les Pétrarquistes*', *Modern Philology*, 28 (1930–31), pp. 1–11.

E. Golenistcheff-Koutouzoff, 'La Première Traduction des "Triomphes" de Pétrarque en France', in *Mélanges offerts à Henri Hauvette* (Paris, 1934), pp. 107–12.

R. Griffiths, 'Some uses of Petrarchan imagery in sixteenth-century France', *French Studies*, 18 (1964), pp. 311–21.

H. Hauvette, *Luigi Alamanni: un exilé florentin à la cour de France au XVIᵉ siècle* . . . (Paris, 1903).

—— *Les Poésies lyriques de Pétrarque* (Paris, 1931).

R. Lebègue, 'Un Volume de vers italiens annotés par Ronsard', *Bulletin du bibliophile* (1951), pp. 273–80.

C. A. Mayer, 'Clément Marot and Literary History', in *Studies in French Literature Presented to H. W. Lawton* (Manchester, 1968), pp. 247–60.

C. A. Mayer, with D. Bentley-Cranch, 'Le Premier Pétrarquiste français, Jean Marot', *Bibliothèque d'Humanisme et Renaissance,* 27 (1965), pp. 183–5.

—— 'Clément Marot, poète pétrarquiste', *Bibliothèque d'Humanisme et Renaissance*, 28 (1966), pp. 32–51.

N. Mann, 'Pierre Flamenc, admirateur de Pétrarque', *Romania*, 91 (1970), pp. 306–40.

E. Ornato, 'La prima fortuna del Petrarca in Francia', *Studi francesi*, 5 (1961), pp. 201–17 and 401–14.

A. Pauphilet, 'Sur des vers de Pétrarque', in *Mélanges offerts à Henri Hauvette* (Paris, 1934), pp. 113–21.

C. Pellegrini, 'Il Petrarca nella cultura francese', in *Tradizione italiana e cultura europea* (Messina, 1947), pp. 5–18.

M. Piéri, *Le Pétrarquisme au XVIᵉ siècle: Pétrarque et Ronsard ou de l'influence de Pétrarque sur la Pléiade française* (Marseille, 1896).

É. Picot, *Les Italiens en France au XVIᵉ siècle* (Bordeaux, 1901–2).

—— *Des Français qui ont écrit en italien au XVIᵉ siècle* (Paris, 1902).

—— *Les Français italianisants au XVIᵉ siècle*, two vols (Paris, 1906–7).

E. M. Rutson, 'A note on Jean Marot's debt to Italian sources', *Modern Language Review*, 61 (1966), pp. 25–8.

C. Ruutz-Rees, 'A note on Saint-Gelais and Bembo', *Romanic Review,* 1 (1910), pp. 427–9.

F. Simone, 'Il Petrarca e la cultura francese del suo tempo', *Studi francesi*, 14 (1970), pp. 201–15 and 403–17.

G. Spagnoletti, *Il Petrarchismo* (Milan, 1959).

J. Vianey, *Le Pétrarquisme en France au XVIᵉ siècle* (Paris, 1909).

M. White, 'Petrarchism in the French rondeau before 1527',

French Studies, 22 (1968), pp. 287–95.

E. H. Wilkins, 'A general survey of Renaissance Petrarchism', *Comparative Literature*, 2 (1950), pp. 327–42.

—— *The Making of the 'Canzoniere' and other Petrarchan Studies* (Rome, 1951).

—— *Studies in the Life and Works of Petrarch* (Cambridge, Massachusetts, 1955).

—— *The Invention of the Sonnet and other Studies in Italian Literature* (Rome, 1959).

French literature and the European background
(a) *Texts*

J. du Bellay, *Œuvres poétiques*, ed. H. Chamard, six vols (Paris, 1908–31). All quotations are taken from this edition.

—— *La Deffence et illustration de la langue françoyse*, ed. H. Chamard (Paris, 1948).

—— *L'Olive*, ed. E. Caldarini (Geneva, 1974).

Bernard de Ventadour, *Chansons d'Amour*, ed. M. Lazar (Paris, 1966).

S. Champier, *Le Livre de vraye amour*, ed. J. B. Wadsworth (The Hague, 1962).

Charles d'Orléans, *Poésies*, ed. P. Champion, two vols (Paris, 1923–24).

The Poetical Works of Alain Chartier, ed. J. C. Laidlaw (Cambridge, 1974). All quotations are taken from this edition.

Documents inédits sur l'histoire de France: Recueil d'Arts de Seconde Rhétorique, ed. E. Langlois (Paris, 1902).

P. Fabri, *Le Grand et Vrai Art de pleine rhétorique*, ed. A. Héron, three vols (Rouen, 1889–90).

Chansons de Gace Brulé, ed. G. Huet (Paris, 1902).

A. Héroët, *Œuvres poétiques*, ed. F. Gohin (Paris, 1909).

Le Jardin de plaisance et fleur de rhétorique, two vols (Paris, 1910–25). Vol 1: reproduction of the text of the original edition. Vol. 2: introduction and notes by E. Droz and A. Piaget.

L. Labé, *Sonnets*, ed. and trans. P. Sharratt and G. D. Martin, Edinburgh Bilingual Library (Edinburgh, 1973).

J. Lemaire de Belges, *Œuvres complètes*, ed. J. Stecher, four vols (Louvain, 1882–85).

C. Marot, *Œuvres complètes*, ed. A. Grenier, two vols (Paris, 1938).

—— *Les Epîtres*, ed. C. A. Mayer (London, 1958).

—— *Œuvres satiriques*, ed. Mayer (London, 1962).

—— *Œuvres lyrinques*, ed. Mayer (London, 1964).

—— *Œuvres diverses*, ed. Mayer (London, 1966).

—— *Les Épigrammes*, ed. Mayer (London, 1970).

All quotations from Marot are taken from the Mayer edition.

J. Moderne, *Le Parangon des chansons*, nine books (Lyon, 1538–41). I have used British Library copy K. 10. a. 9.

J. Molinet, *Les Faictz et ditz*, ed. N. Dupire, three vols (Paris, 1936–39).

J. Peletier de Mans, *Art Poëtique*, ed. A. Boulanger (Paris, 1930).

Pernette du Guillet, *Rymes*, ed. V. E. Graham (Geneva, 1968).

Pontus de Tyard, *Œuvres poétiques complètes*, ed. J. C. Lapp (Paris, 1966).

Le Roman de la Rose, ed. E. Langlois, five vols (Paris, 1914–24). All quotations are taken from this edition.

P. de Ronsard, *Œuvres complètes*, edited by P. Laumonier, 18 vols. (Paris, 1931–67). This edition was completed by I. Silver and R. Lebègue.

—— *Les Amours* edited by H. Weber and C. Weber (Paris, 1963). All quotations are taken from this edition.

M. de Saint-Gelais, *Œuvres complètes*, ed. P. Blanchemain, three vols. (Paris, 1973). A modern critical edition is badly needed.

T. Sebillet, *Art poétique françoys*, ed. F. Gaiffe (Paris, 1932).

F. Villon, *Œuvres*, ed. A. Longnon and L. Foulet, fourth edition (Paris, 1966).

(b) Critical studies

R. R. Bezzola, 'Guillaume IX et les origines de l'amour courtois', *Romania*, 66 (1940), pp. 145(237.

—— *Les Origines et la formation de la littérature courtoise en occident (500–1200)*, three parts (Paris, 1944–63).

G. Castor, *Pléiade Poetics* (Cambridge, 1964).

T. Cave, ed., *Ronsard the Poet* (London, 1973).

H. Chamard, *Joachim du Bellay* (Lille, 1900).

—— *Les Origines de la poésie française de la Renaissance* (Paris, 1920).

—— *Histoire de la Pléiade*, four vols (Paris, 1961). First published in 1939.

P. Champion, 'Du succès de l'œuvre de Charles d'Orléans et de ses imitateurs jusqu'au XVIe siècle, in *Mélanges offerts à Émile Picot*, two vols (Paris, 1913), 1, 409–20.

E. R. Curtius, *European Literature and the Latin Middle Ages*, trans. W. R. Trask (New York, 1953).

M. Dassonville, 'Pour une interprétation nouvelle des *Amours* de Ronsard', *Bibliothèque d'Humanisme et Renaissance*, 28 (1966), pp. 241–70.

F. Desonay, *Ronsard, poète de l'amour*, three vols (Brussels, 1952–59).

G. Dottin, 'Aspects littéraires de la chanson "musicale" à l'époque de Marot', *Revue des Sciences Humaines* (1964), pp. 425–32.

P. Dronke, *Medieval Latin and the Rise of European Love-Lyric*, second edition, two vols (Oxford, 1968).

―― *The Medieval Lyric* (London, 1968).

J. Fox, *The Lyric Poetry of Charles d'Orléans* (Oxford, 1969).

―― *A Literary History of France: The Middle Ages* (London and New York, 1974).

M. Françon, 'Notes sur l'histoire du sonnet en France', *Italica*, 29 (1952), pp. 121–8.

―― 'Sur le premier sonnet français publié', *Bibliothèque d'Humanisme et Renaissance*, 33 (1971), pp. 365–6.

A. Gendre, *Ronsard, poète de la conquête amoureuse* (Neuchâtel, 1970).

L. E. Harvey, *The Aesthetics of the Renaissance Love Sonnet: An Essay on the Art of the Sonnet in the Poetry of Louise Labé* (Geneva, 1962).

D. Heartz, *Pierre Attaingnant, Royal Printer of Music: a Historical Study and Bibliographical Catalogue* (Berkeley, California, 1969).

C. A. Mayer, 'Ronsard et Molinet', *Bibliothèque d'Humanisme et Renaissance*, 26 (1964), pp. 417–18.

―― 'Le Premier Sonnet français: Marot, Mellin de Saint-Gelais et Jean Bouchet', *Revue d'histoire littéraire de la France*, 67 (1967), pp. 481–93.

C. A. Mayer and P. M. Smith, 'La Première Épigramme française: Clément Marot, Jean Bouchet et Michel d'Amboise—Définition, sources, antériorité', *Bibliothèque d'Humanisme et Renaissance*, 32 (1970), pp. 579–602.

H.-J. Molinier, *Mellin de Saint-Gelays* (Rodez, 1910).

W. F. Patterson, *Three Centuries of French Poetic Theory*, two vols (Ann Arbor, Michigan, 1935).

S. F. Pogue, *Jacques Moderne, Lyons Music Printer of the Sixteenth Century* (Geneva, 1969).

D. Poirion, *Le Poète et le prince: l'évolution du lyrisme courtois de Guillaume de Machaut à Charles d'Orléans* (Paris, 1965).

M. Raymond. *L'Influence de Ronsard sur la poésie française 1550–1585*, second edition (Geneva, 1965).

C. Ruutz Rees, *Charles de Sainte-Marthe* (New York, 1910).

G. Saba, *La poesia di Joachim du Bellay* (Messina and Florence, 1962).

V.-L. Saulnier, 'Étude sur Pernette du Guillet et ses *Rymes*', *Bibliothèque d'Humanisme et Renaissance*, 4 (1944), pp. 7–119.

―― *Du Bellay* (Paris, 1951).

A. H. Schutz, *Vernacular Books in Parisian Private Libraries of the Sixteenth Century according to the Notarial Inventories* (Chapel Hill, North Carolina, 1955).

I. Silver, *The Intellectual Evolution of Ronsard* (St. Louis, Missouri, 1969–). Two volumes have appeared so far.

F. Simone, *Il rinascimento francese* (Turin, 1961). A translation of most of part one of Simone's book, with modification of the notes, has been made by H. Gaston Hall, *The French Renaissance* (London, 1969).

P. M. Smith, *Clément Marot* (London, 1970).

D. Stone, jr, *Ronsard's Sonnet Cycles: A Study in Tone and Vision* (New Haven and London, 1966).

L. Terreaux, 'Ronsard correcteur de ses alexandrins dans les "Hymes" de 1555–1556: le problème de la césure et de l'enjambement', *Cahiers de l'Association Internationale des Etudes Françaises*, 22 (1970), pp. 83–98.

H. Vaganay, *Le Sonnet en Italie et en France au XVIe siècle*, two vols (Lyon, 1903).

M. J. Valency, *In Praise of Love* (New York, 1958).

J. B. Wadsworth, *Lyons 1473–1503: The Beginnings of Cosmopolitanism* (Cambridge, Massachusetts, 1962).

H. Weber, 'Platonisme et sensualité dans la poésie amoureuse de la Pléiade', in *Lumières de la Pléiade* (Paris, 1966), pp. 157–194.

D. B. Wilson, *Ronsard, Poet of Nature* (Manchester, 1961).

P. Zumthor, 'Charles d'Orléans et le langage de l'allégorie', in *Mélanges offerts à Rita Lejeune*, two vols (Gembloux, 1969), pp. 1481–502.